Hamlyn

Ray P.

Trees of the world

illustrated by Karel Tholé
& Ross Wardle

Hamlyn · London
Sun Books · Melbourne

FOREWORD

The purpose of this book is to inform ordinary people about trees and it is hoped that it may add interest to that walk or drive in the country, that stroll in the park or even just to sitting in the garden.

It is not for botanists but for the man, or woman, who calls an oak an oak and not a *Quercus*. Accordingly, the arrangement of this book is based on everyday usage rather than the systems of botanists. Most people think of trees as belonging to the forest, the garden or the orchard, and those are the broad classifications used here.

Popular or common English names are employed rather than Latin ones but the botanists' Latin is also given in parenthesis because that is the only definite and precise means of identification. Popular names do have a rather unfortunate habit of changing from one country to another, even from one district to another. However, the index should help to take care of that problem.

There are thousands and thousands of different trees in the world so for every one mentioned here there must be many omitted, but if this little book leads you to look on one single tree as an old friend, it will not have failed.

R.P.

Published by The Hamlyn Publishing Group Limited
London · New York · Sydney · Toronto
Hamlyn House, Feltham, Middlesex, England
In association with Sun Books Pty. Ltd. Melbourne

ISBN 0 600 10070 7
Photoset by BAS Printers Limited, Wallop, Hampshire
Colour separations by Schwitter Limited, Zurich
Printed in Holland by Smeets, Weert

CONTENTS

WHAT IS A TREE?

A tree seedling looks so much like any other tiny plant that it is difficult to realize that it may grow into one of the largest living organisms in the world. When it does grow up one has no hesitation in calling it a tree but it is not so easy to define what is meant.

A tree is a perennial, like so many other plants: it continues season after season. Its shoots are woody and do not die down in winter, but that applies to shrubs too. Where a tree is unique is that it has, or is capable of having, a single, persistent, woody main stem or trunk.

Most of the trees may be divided into three classes: the broad-leaved (such as the Beech), the conifers with their narrow leaves (such as Norway Spruce) and the palms. Examples of these classes are illustrated opposite.

Most of the broad-leaved trees are deciduous, dropping their leaves once a year. Most of the conifers are evergreen – which does not mean that their leaves are everlasting but that, as they stay on the tree for two years or more, the tree is never bare in spite of regular leaf renewal.

The palms are a rather special class and, except for the Date Palm, not dealt with in this book.

We need not delve deeply into the complexities of botanic classification and nomenclature here but for the benefit of the uninitiated it should just be explained that plants with a number of common characteristics are grouped together in one genus (plural, genera). Thus, there are a number of kinds of oak tree but they all have acorns and all belong to the genus *Quercus*.

Each different kind of oak occurring in nature is called a species and the species epithet forms the second part of the Latin name; for example *Quercus lusitanica* is the oak which comes from Lusitania or Portugal. We shall follow the convention in which the common names of species, but not of larger groups, are capitalized.

Sometimes one species has been crossed with another and the result is a hybrid. Where such plants have been given Latin names they are preceded by the letter 'x'. Thus *Quercus x kewensis* means a hybrid oak raised at Kew.

A broad-leaved tree — an oak

A conifer — the Norway Spruce

A palm — the Date Palm

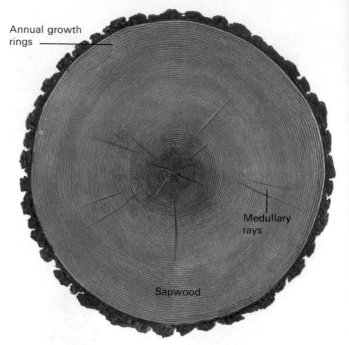

Annual growth rings

Medullary rays

Sapwood

Cross-section through trunk

HOW TREES GROW

The roots of a tree have two functions: to act as anchors and to collect moisture with the mineral salts which may be dissolved in it.

Certain trees living in arid regions have more growth below ground than above but more usually the roots extend horizontally as far as, or only a little more than, the branches above and do not delve as deep as the trunk may soar above ground. Mostly the feeding roots lie in the top 18 inches where the soil is richest. The deeper roots are for anchorage.

The circulatory system of moisture from the root-hairs through the roots and up the sapwood to the leaves and then down through the phloem just beneath the bark, eventually back to the roots, is called translocation. This process is still not fully understood. Partly it is due to transpiration, the loss of moisture by evaporation from the leaf pores, being made good by suction, partly it may be due to capillary attraction and partly there is a definite pressure created by the roots for, if a tree is cut down, the stump will bleed.

In temperate regions tree growth follows a regular annual pattern, more porous wood being made in spring to satisfy the greater demand for moisture at that season and more fibrous wood, darker in colour, being made later. These differences produce the familiar annual rings. In tropical areas growth may be almost continuous so that there are no obvious annual rings, or where rainy seasons are interspersed with dry periods, more than one may be made in a year.

At the centre of a cross-section of tree trunk is found the heartwood. This was once sapwood but has become compressed, stronger, probably darker in colour and impregnated with tannin in broad-leaved trees, or resin in conifers.

Around the heartwood is the sapwood through which sap is drawn up from the roots. The sap does not rise in spring and fall in autumn: it merely circulates more rapidly in spring and summer.

The heartwood and the sapwood together form the xylem –

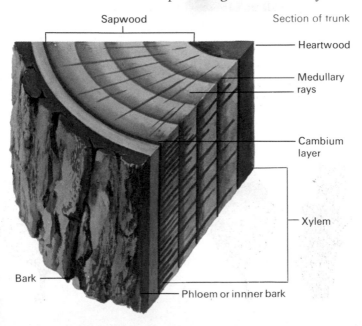

Section of trunk

Sapwood

Heartwood

Medullary rays

Cambium layer

Xylem

Bark

Phloem or innner bark

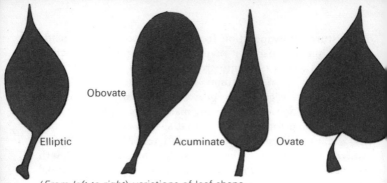

Obovate

Elliptic

Acuminate

Ovate

(*From left to right*) variations of leaf shape

what most people would just call 'wood' – and radiating out approximately from the centre and crossing the annual rings at right angles will be seen a few faint broken lines looking rather like hair-thin cracks. These are the medullary rays in which nutrient material is stored and carried horizontally through the xylem.

Around the outside of the most recent ring of sapwood there is a one-cell thick strip called the cambium layer. This is the part of the tree which really manufactures new growth. The cells divide and those on the inner side form xylem and those on the outer add to the next outer layer, called the phloem.

This is a vital area. When the moisture and minerals reach the leaves they are there acted upon by the sun. In a process known as photosynthesis the raw materials are converted into carbohydrates and then distributed via the phloem. Protecting

(*From left to right*) variations in the leaf edge or margin

Scale-like

Ciliate

Crenate

Entire

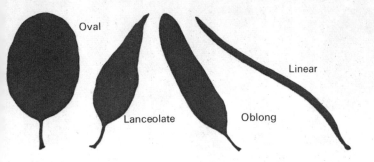

Oval

Lanceolate

Oblong

Linear

the phloem there is the familiar outer skin, the bark.

Some trees propagate vegetatively, by suckers, aerial roots or from portions which break off and root as cuttings. The most usual method, both in nature and under man's control, is by seed. All trees produce flowers, even the conifers.

For the production of seed, fertilization is necessary by pollen. Often the male and female organs occur in the same flower. In other trees there are two types of flower, a female seed-carrying one, and a male pollen-bearing one. Such a tree is said to be monoecious, a word deriving from the Greek meaning 'living in one house'.

Finally, there are trees which are dioecious, meaning 'living in separate houses'. These trees have either male or female flowers, but never both. In such cases where the fruits are wanted, the tree's sex must be known and one of the opposite sex planted nearby.

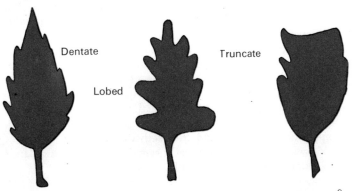

Dentate

Lobed

Truncate

Felled timber being hauled away by tractor

WHERE TREES GROW

Trees occupy about a quarter of the Earth's land area and have
adapted themselves to a very wide range of conditions. There
are species that will flourish in relative dryness, others which
grow in swamps. Some will survive heat and heavy rain, but
none will live in the cold higher or upper altitudes, and none
in the deserts.

Nature provides for the continuation of the species with a
lavishness that is necessary where the odds against survival
are so great. A single birch tree is said to bear a million seeds
at a time while only one in fifty years may be needed to
replace its parent. Nevertheless the dice are so heavily loaded
against the tree seedling that, if a forest is completely cleared,
competing vegetation and the teeth of animals in search of
food will probably ensure that it remains thus. The highlands
of Scotland are such an example.

In managed forests, where trees are felled only as they reach maturity, natural regeneration can be employed, but even then the self-sown seedlings need man's protection. This is common practice in Europe and tropical countries.

After wholesale felling, however, replacement is necessary by more artificial means. The seeds are then germinated where the seedlings may be nursed through infancy before being planted in place of the trees that have been cut.

For centuries, man has taken forest land as he wanted it – for grazing cattle, for growing crops, for minerals and for buildings and towns – with never a thought of reinstating what he has taken. Only recently has it been realized that there is not an inexhaustible area of forest to plunder.

Man has long recognized the wonder of a living tree and has planted trees in gardens for pleasure. Now the value of trees is appreciated in conserving water supplies, preventing flooding and checking soil erosion. In more enlightened countries the planting of hedges and trees to occupy a certain proportion of the land is compulsory by law.

Transplanting seedling trees in a nursery. The portable screen protects them against the drying wind

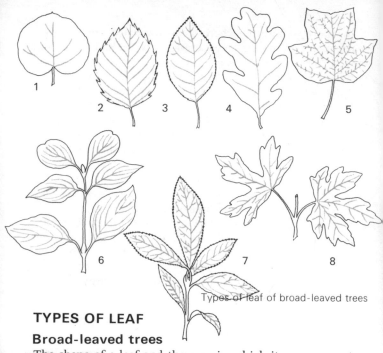

Types of leaf of broad-leaved trees

TYPES OF LEAF
Broad-leaved trees

The shape of a leaf and the way in which it grows on a tree can provide helpful clues to identification. The leaves of all broad-leaved trees are either simple, that is occurring singly, or compound, when each leaf has two or more leaflets. Whether simple or compound, leaves may be either opposite, arising in pairs on opposite sides of the stem or twig, or alternate, in which they originate at different levels although many alternate leaves do in fact spring from very nearly the same level. In some genera, also, different types of leaf may be borne on the same tree or in different species and these have been omitted from the examples below, unless specially mentioned.

Leaves with a smooth edge, not toothed, are said to be entire. Pinnate means arranged in pairs from a common stalk, herringbone fashion, like a feather. Thus, opposite leaflets in a compound leaf are pinnate. The lobes of a leaf can be arranged pinnately, and so too can the veins.

Simple alternate leaves: *Entire;* Eucalyptus (when adult),

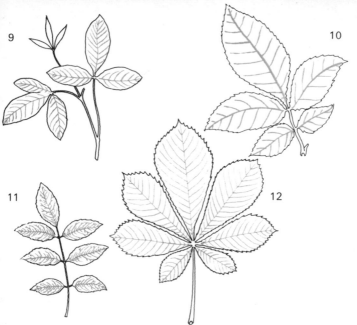

Judas Tree [Fig. 1], Magnolia, Persimmon, Quince. *Toothed;* as there are many examples of this type they may be further sub-divided into – *With dry fruit;* Alder [Fig. 2], Balsa, Beech, Birch, Elm, Hornbeam, Lime, Nut, Poplar, Sweet Chestnut. *With fleshy fruit;* Apple [Fig. 3], Hawthorn (May), Holly (but higher leaves can be entire), Medlar, Mulberry, Pear, the genus *Prunus* (which includes Almond, Cherry, Laurel, Peach and Plum), Strawberry Tree, Whitebeam. *Pinnately lobed;* Oak [Fig. 4]. *Palmate;* (lobes arranged like fingers of the hand); Fig, Liquidambar, Plane, Sycamore, Tulip Tree [Fig. 5].

Simple opposite leaves: *Entire;* Box, Cape Chestnut, Catalpa, Dogwood, Eucalyptus (while juvenile), Lilac [Fig. 6], Mangrove, Olive, Sandalwood, Teak. *Toothed;* Spindle Tree [Fig. 7]. *Palmate;* Maple (that is Acers, except Box Elder which has pinnate leaves) [Fig. 8].

Compound alternate leaves: *Entire;* False Acacia, Laburnum [Fig. 9]. *Toothed;* Hickory [Fig. 10], Mountain Ash, Pepper Tree, Service Tree, Walnut.

Compound opposite leaves: *Pinnate;* Ash [Fig. 11], Elder, Box Elders, Lignum Vitae. *Palmate;* Horse Chestnut [Fig. 12].

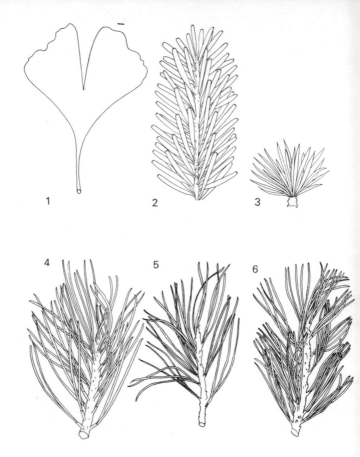

1   2   3

4   5   6

Conifers

With the special exception of the Maidenhair Tree [Fig. 1],
which has flat-bladed leaves like a broad-leaved tree, the
conifers have either linear or scale-like leaves lying close to
the shoot. The linear leaves are the more common and they
may be quite thin and needle-like or comparatively broad
although still long, if less pointed. To aid in identification, the
conifers may be divided into the following groups:

Thin, linear leaves or needles: *Borne singly;* Douglas Fir,
Fir [Fig. 2], Juniper, Podocarpus, Spruce. *Borne in tufts of two*
[Fig. 4], *three* [Fig. 5], *five* [Fig. 6] *and, very occasionally, six*

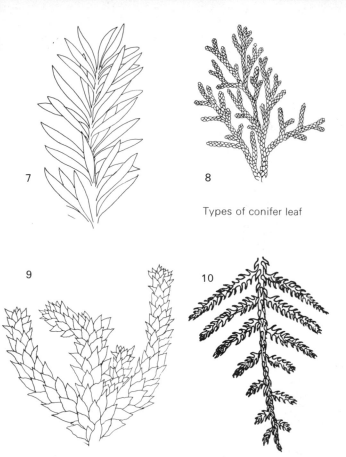

Types of conifer leaf

needles per cluster; All pines except the species *Pinus cem-broides monophylla* in which the leaves are borne singly. *Borne in clusters on short shoots;* Cedar, Larch [Fig. 3].

Linear but broader leaves, not needles: *Leaves borne singly and alternately;* Fossil Tree, Hemlock, Redwood, Swamp Cypress, Yew [Fig. 7].

Scale-like: *Leaves quite small and overlapping;* True and False Cypress [Fig. 8], Rimu, Thuja. *Leaves large, arranged spirally;* Monkey Puzzle [Fig. 9]. *Leaves small, densely arranged, individually awl-shaped* (tapering from base to apex); Norfolk Island Pine [Fig. 10], Wellingtonia.

TYPES OF FLOWER

A catkin is a pendulous spike of stalkless, unisexual flowers. Pollen is transferred from the male flowers to the female by the wind. The alder, birch, hazel, poplar and willow are common trees having catkins. (*Left*) male and female catkins of the Common Alder and (*below left*) catkins of the Common Hazel.

Catkins

Spike

Catkins

(*Above*) spikes of Golden Wattle. These are single stemmed flower clusters in which the flowers themselves are stalkless, or nearly so. This term is sometimes used rather loosely for any long, thin raceme. Spikes are found more commonly on shrubs rather than trees. Another example is the Prickly Wattle.

A panicle is a raceme (*see below*) in which branches spring from the central stem, each carrying stalked flowers. The laterals themselves may branch and as the largest branches are at the base, the whole cluster has a pyramidal shape. The Horse Chestnut (*right*) has erect panicles.

A raceme is an unbranched cluster of flowers, each of which is attached by a stalk to the central stem. An example is the Laburnum (below), in which the racemes are pendulous.

Panicle

Raceme

Umbel

An umbel is a cluster of flowers, the stalks of which all originate from the same point, as in cherries and eucalyptus. It is also possible to have a compound umbel in which the stalks of a number of umbels, or clusters, originate from the same point on the main stem. (*Right*) an umbel of cherry blossom (*top*) and (*below*) a compound umbel of the Mediterranean shrub *Bupleurum fruticosum*.

Compound umbel

FOREST TREES – BROAD-LEAVED

Acacia (Wattle)

This is a genus of over 500 species, mostly natives of Australia, although also widely grown in many of the warmer areas of both hemispheres.

Many species are shrubs rather than trees, and most are evergreen, the leaves being bipinnate. In some species juvenile leaves give place to phyllodes, which are leaf-like expansions of the stalk, anything from 1 to 12 inches in length, more able to resist drought. Flowers are usually yellow, sometimes white.

Acacia catechu originated in India and the East Indies. It yields catechu used in tanning. *A. decurrens,* the Green Wattle, which flowers in spring, and its variety *mollissima* (or *mearnsii*) the Black Wattle, which flowers in summer, are

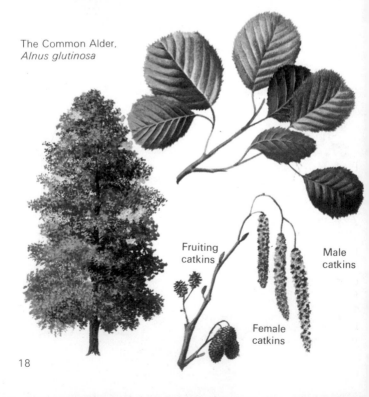

The Common Alder,
Alnus glutinosa

Fruiting catkins

Male catkins

Female catkins

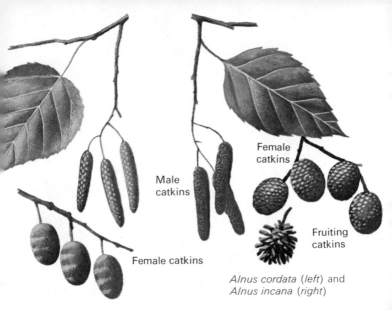

Male catkins

Female catkins

Female catkins

Fruiting catkins

Alnus cordata (*left*) and
Alnus incana (*right*)

widely grown in Australia and South Africa, the bark being used in tanning.

The Australian Blackwood, *A. melanoxylon,* grows to 80 feet and produces timber in demand for furniture because of the beauty of its 'fiddleback' figuring. Particularly pretty is *A. pycnantha,* the Golden Wattle of Victoria, a small tree with notably fragrant flowers.

A. senegal is to be found in tropical Africa and, appropriately, in some parts of the Arabian peninsula – it yields gum arabic. (See also *Acacia,* page 90, and False Acacia, page 35).

Alder (Alnus)

The Common Alder or Black Alder (*Alnus glutinosa*), native of Britain, Europe, north Africa and Asia Minor, is widely cultivated in other temperate regions. The male catkins develop in autumn and hang on the tree until the female flowers, looking like miniature fir cones, appear in spring. The latter remain on the tree, after the seed has fallen from them, through the winter. The leaves are hairy and sticky when young and remain green late into the fall.

The Common Ash,
Fraxinus excelsior

Flower cluster

Detail of leaf

Young fruits or 'keys'

Mature fruits

Flower buds

Alder timber was once prized for making the best charcoal for gunpowder and for the soles of the Lancashire weavers' clogs. Durable when submerged, the wood was used for early water-pipes. The alder is a good tree to grow for the prevention of river bank erosion and has the added merit of tolerating salt water.

Other widely-grown species include *A. cordata* from Corsica and Italy, a handsome tree with the largest fruits of all the alders, and *A. incana,* the Grey Alder, known in America as the Speckled Alder. The latter has smooth, grey bark and a number of cut-leaved varieties.

Ash (Fraxinus)

Grown in Britain, Europe, north Africa and western Asia, the Common Ash (*Fraxinus excelsior*) is one of Europe's tallest and most graceful native trees. Not very long-lived, it grows rapidly and in favourable circumstances reaches a height of 140 feet. Etymologists say that its name derives from the Saxon and does not refer to the ash-grey colour of the bark. At an early age the bark becomes fissured and often grows lichens too which make the tree appear old.

In early spring the black buds are very noticeable. The leaves are borne in opposite pairs. They are about a foot long and have from three to seven (usually four or five) pairs of lance-shaped, toothed leaflets with a singleton at the tip. The Ash is normally one of the last trees to produce its leaves in spring (and the first to lose them) but, according to the old English proverb, if the Oak comes out before the Ash, the earth will only get a splash, but if the Ash precedes the Oak, then it is in for a soak. Curiously, these weather signs are reversed in Cornwall and north Germany.

The tiny purplish flowers develop in clusters, before the leaves, but having neither calyx nor corolla are rather insignificant. It seems that insects also tend to ignore them and fertilization is performed by the wind. The fruits grow in bunches of flat 'wings', popularly called 'keys'. Each key has a seed at one end and a slight twist in its length ensures that when it flutters to the ground it spins and falls seed-end first. These keys used to be pickled and John Evelyn, the diarist, said they 'afford a delicate salading'.

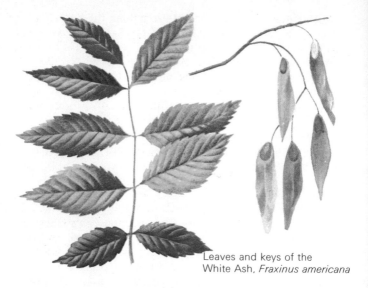

Leaves and keys of the
White Ash, *Fraxinus americana*

The wood is tough and elastic and very suitable for hockey sticks and the handles of tools such as axes. Ash is popular too, for walking sticks, the growing of which is a specialized business. Young plants are cut back, dug up and replanted at an angle so that, when fresh vertical growth is made from a side bud, the stick is provided with a handle.

The White Ash (*Fraxinus americana*) is a native of the eastern states of the United States where it reaches a height of 120 feet. It is similar to the Common Ash but its petal-less flowers are white. It was introduced to Britain in 1724.

The Manna Ash (*Fraxinus ornus*), known in America as the Flowering Ash and a popular tree in New Zealand, originated in southern Europe and Asia Minor. It received its name from the sugary gum that oozes in summer from cuts in the bark and was supposed to resemble the miraculous desert food of the Israelites.

The Desert Ash (*Fraxinus oxycarpa*) grows to about 30 feet but withstands relatively dry conditions and is used for street planting in Australia. Very similar is the Narrow-leaved Ash (*Fraxinus angustifolia*) which grows taller and has glossy leaves, those of the Desert Ash always being downy.

Aspen (Populus)

The Aspen or Trembling Poplar (*Populus tremula*) known in America as the European Aspen is widely distributed in the temperate regions of the northern hemisphere. The upper surfaces of the leaves are dark green, while the lower surfaces are paler. They hang downwards, the stalks being too long and thin to hold them horizontally, and thus they quiver in the slightest breeze.

The American Aspen, also known as the Quaking Aspen (*Populus tremuloides*), may be distinguished from its European cousin by the pale yellowish colour of the bark in youth and its smaller, finely-toothed leaves. It is said to be the only Californian tree to grow as far north as the Arctic Circle (see also Poplar, page 60).

Balsa (Ochroma)

The Balsa (*Ochroma lagopus*) is an evergreen tree of tropical America growing to a height of 60 feet in a few years. Its wood is extremely light as any schoolboy who has ever made a model aircraft knows. One cubic foot dried in the air weighs only 6 to 12 pounds.

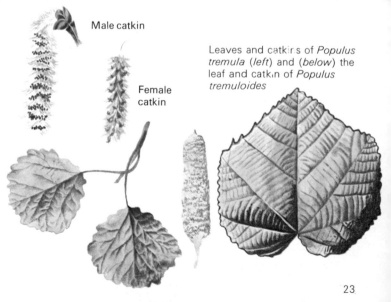

Male catkin

Female catkin

Leaves and catkins of *Populus tremula* (*left*) and (*below*) the leaf and catkin of *Populus tremuloides*

Beech (Fagus)

The Common Beech (*Fagus sylvatica*) is a native of western Asia and all Europe as far as southern England. Many were planted in the eighteenth century to improve the landscape for the big English estates.

Beech flourishes best on chalky soil. Good specimens reach from 100 to 150 feet, the straight stems being surmounted by a rounded, spreading crown. The curious shapes of some English beech trees in the New Forest and around the Chilterns are quite unnatural, the result of pollarding in youth.

Beech trees do not root deeply and much of the main roots may be seen above the ground. They are deciduous and in late winter their twigs are distinctive by reason of their long, pointed brown buds. The leaves are alternate and when they open in spring it will be seen that they have been folded like miniature fans and at first they have a delicate fringe of hairs at the edge.

The male, pollen-bearing flowers occur as clusters of three

or four, round in shape, brownish in colour, drooping from slender stalks. The female flowers are on stouter stems and cluster within a bristly green 'cupule'. In the autumn these cupules split into four and the reflex segments reveal the three-sided nuts commonly known as beech mast.

Beech mast is rich in oil and was once freely used in pig-feeding. The oil has been used for making a butter substitute and a scheme was once proposed for paying off the British national debt with the proceeds of beech nut oil. This is reminiscent of the ill-fated groundnut scheme.

In autumn the leaves turn colour but continue to hang on the lower, younger branches through the winter, a feature which makes beech a popular subject for hedges where regular cutting ensures a regular succession of young growth. Beech leaves were once used to stuff mattresses. Evelyn said they were superior to straw because they would 'continue sweet for seven or eight years'. The branches of beech trees

(*Opposite*) an avenue of Common Beech, *Fagus sylvatica*, and (*below*) detail of leaf, bark and fruit of the Common Beech

Bark

Cupule

Fruit

have a marked tendency to join together where they cross by chance, forming natural grafts.

A distinctive feature of the beech is its smooth, grey bark which since Roman times has invited youthful knife-owners to commemorate themselves and their loves. There is a story – but only a story, unfortunately – that printing had its origin in the experiments of a citizen of Haarlem in Holland who, to amuse his grandchildren, printed verses from letters incised on beech bark.

Beech wood is not very durable in the open but it is strong and has a high reputation for turning and furniture-making. It is exceptionally good for bending under the influence of steam.

Truffles – underground fungi, prized by gourmets for their exquisite flavour – sometimes grow in beech woods. They have a strong scent and both pigs and dogs have been trained as pointers to these subterranean delicacies.

There are several varieties of *Fagus sylvatica* grown for the beauty of their leaves. The variety *cuprea,* the Copper Beech, is thought to have been a sport from *purpurea,* the Purple Beech (itself a sport of *F. sylvatica*), five trees of which, it was recorded in 1680, had grown up on the spot in Switzerland where five brothers had murdered one another.

Searching for truffles in beech wood. Inset of truffle

Fruit

Cupule

(*Left*) leaves, fruit and cupule of the American Beech, *Fagus grandifolia*. (*Right*) a southern hemisphere beech, *Nothofagus cunninghamii*, an evergreen species

The American Beech (*Fagus grandifolia*), a native of North America, has been tried in Britain but without much success. It can be distinguished from Common Beech by its longer, narrower leaves with more veins and its ability to spread by producing suckers.

The southern hemisphere has its own particular race of beeches known as *Nothofagus*, which means 'false beech'. The fact that these originated in South America, Australia, Tasmania and New Zealand has been taken as evidence that these land masses were once all joined. Several species are evergreen including *N. cunninghamii* which reaches 200 feet in its native Tasmania and the popular Red Beech (*N. fusca*), of New Zealand, which can exceed 100 feet. Considerable quantities of the pale salmon-pink timber of another evergreen, the Silver Beech (*N. menziesii*) are exported from its native New Zealand.

Birch (Betula)

The birches are graceful trees of the north temperate and arctic regions. Deciduous, they have alternate, toothed leaves and bear male and female catkins on the same tree. They favour light, sandy soils. Distinctive characteristics of the birches are their spidery branches and twigs which make them particularly beautiful in winter and their curiously papery and often very pretty bark.

The Silver Birch or European White Birch (*Betula pendula*), native of Asia Minor and Europe, is typical. It grows to 50 or 60 feet, its silvery bark tends to peel and the branch ends to hang down. The twigs are smooth but warty. The male catkins form in autumn and turn red in spring when the shorter, green female catkins emerge at the same time as the leaves. The male catkins then shrivel and fall, while the female ones grow as the tiny winged fruits within develop until they burst out in the autumn. There are some horticultural varieties including a purple-leaved one.

The Canoe or Paper Bark Birch (*B. papyrifera*) is a native of North America. Its peeling, papery bark is white and was used by Red Indians in the making of canoes, as well as for roofing and drinking utensils.

Silver Birch, *Betula pendula*, (*left*) with details of leaves and catkins

Female (fruiting) catkin

Male catkin

Flower

Common Box, *Buxus sempervirens*, (*left*) and (*right*) example of the topiary work for which box is often used

Box (Buxus)

The one-time popularity of dwarf box hedges in gardens and the use of this subject for training and clipping in the shape of men, birds, beasts and the other decorative shapes used in the art of topiary, are apt to blind us to the fact that this can be a tree. The Common Box (*Buxus sempervirens*) grows to 20 feet or so in Britain, somewhat higher in parts of Europe. It is a native of England (hence Box Hill in Surrey and Boxley in Kent) and also of southern Europe, western Asia and northern Africa.

The inch-long opposite leaves are evergreen, entire, leathery, with a polished upper surface.

As the box grows extremely slowly, its wood is very dense – it will not float in water – and has a fine grain. It is used for textile rollers, silk shuttles and objects which have to withstand sharp blows – mallets and skittles for instance. Box is used for rulers and mathematical instruments, and was once in demand for printing blocks.

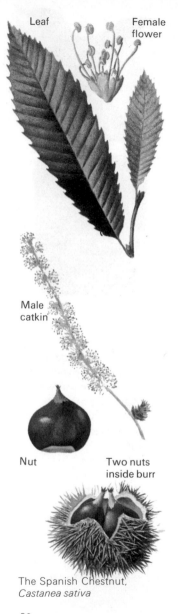

Leaf

Female flower

Male catkin

Nut

Two nuts inside burr

The Spanish Chestnut,
Castanea sativa

Carapa

Carapa is a tropical South American genus. The timber of *Carapa guianensis* is known as crabwood, but sometimes sold as British Guiana or Brazilian mahogany, although darker and harder than true American mahogany. The trees can reach 170 feet in America, only 60 feet in Britain. The leathery leaves are shiny and the fruit as big as an apple.

Chestnut (Castanea)

No relation of the Horse Chestnut (page 42), the Sweet or Spanish Chestnut (*Castanea sativa*) may have originated in Asia Minor but is now common in the north temperate zone. It grows well in Britain, but does not usually produce nuts as large as those of southern Europe. The flowers are pale yellow and the nuts enclosed in prickly burrs or cupules.

It makes a large tree, about 100 feet, with a girth up to 40 feet, the bark developing deep spiral fissures. The toothed, pointed leaves are 5 to 9 inches long and the parallel veins are very noticeable on the upper surface. The wood is like oak but without the silver grain. It is widely used for fencing.

(*Above*) branched cluster of blossoms of the elder *Sambucus nigra* and detail of leaf. (*Left*) berries from which wine is often made, although the fruit of other species is poisonous

Dalbergia

The Dalbergias are tropical evergreens yielding a very hard timber of commercial importance. Brazilian Rosewood (*Dalbergia nigra*) is used for cabinet-making, Honduras Rosewood (*D. stevensonii*) for knife handles and xylophone keys, Indian Rosewood (*D. latifolia*) for furniture and dance floors, Sissoo (*D. sissoo*) for railway sleepers.

Elder (Sambucus)

Most of the elders are shrubby but the elder of Europe and Britain (*Sambucus nigra*) can grow to 30 feet. By tradition the tree on which Judas Iscariot hanged himself, it has been the object of superstition. In the past all parts of the tree were thought to have medicinal properties. Today, wine is still made from the berries, but it should be noted that the fruit of some other species is poisonous. The pith is easily removed from younger shoots so that they are often used as pipes, musical instruments and pea-shooters.

English Elms, *Ulmus procera*

Elm (Ulmus)

Native of southern England, western and southern Europe, the English Elm (*Ulmus procera*) is a very tall tree (*procera* means 'very tall'), sometimes reaching 150 feet. The trunk is straight with deep vertical furrows and much of it branchless; the canopy of spreading branches being high from the ground. Freedom from knots, therefore, is a characteristic of elm timber.

The flowers appear before the leaves, inconspicuous reddish tufts close to the twigs. The fruits appear soon after, still before the leaves, and these take the form of semi-transparent discs properly known as 'samara' in each of which a single seed is lodged. These seeds, however, are almost always infertile but the trees sucker freely and these root readily when chiselled off and transplanted.

The leaves of the English Elm are markedly uneven at the base, the leaf extending further one side of the central vein than the other. They are coarsely and doubly toothed and come abruptly to a point. Dark green in colour, they are very rough on the upper surface.

Another European elm, more common in the north and west of England, Scotland and Ireland, is the Wych or Scotch Elm (*U. glabra*). Its leaves are also markedly unequal and the upper surface rough. The species name *glabra,* which means 'smooth', refers to the bark. The trunk up to the first branches is relatively shorter than the English Elm's and it does not produce suckers. The seeds, however, are fertile.

Other common elms in Britain are the Smooth-leaved Elm (*U. carpinifolia*) growing to no more than 100 feet, with rough bark, pink flowers and infertile seeds, and the more slender Plot Elm (*U. plotii*), which has shorter leaf stalks and fewer leaf veins. The leaves of the former species are very unequal at the base, those of the latter nearly equal.

The American or White Elm (*U. americana*) originated in central and eastern North America, where it is one of the finest and most beautiful of trees. It grows to 120 feet and the graceful branches are pendulous at the tip. The leaves are unequal at the base and run to a long, slender tip. The Slippery Elm (*U. fulva*), also from North America, is a smaller

English Elms are usually sterile and propagated by layering

Flowers appear before the leaves

Leaf

Close up of flower

Fruit with seed within

Leaves of some common elms

Wych Elm, *Ulmus glabra*

Smooth-leaved Elm, *Ulmus carpinifolia*

American Elm, *Ulmus americana*

Slippery Elm, *Ulmus fulva*

tree (70 feet). The leaves are downy beneath but extremely rough on top. Its common name refers to the gummy inner bark of the tree.

Elms have the reputation of casting their branches suddenly, without warning but the timber is remarkably durable if kept always dry or always wet. Elm piles used for old Waterloo Bridge were still sound when the bridge was rebuilt more than 120 years later. Elm was often used for water pipes.

Elm burrs are prized by furniture-makers because of the fascinating whorls and twists they give to the figuring of the wood. Effective use of burr elm veneers was made in the panelling of doors, staircases and rooms in the liner Queen Mary.

False Acacia or Locust (Robinia pseudoacacia)

In the three centuries since it was brought from its native North America to France and named after Jean Robin, botanist to Henry IV, king of France, the identity of this tree has been confused by its many names.

Early missionaries in America thought it was the acacia of Egypt which provided John the Baptist with locusts in the wilderness and so they called it the Locust Tree. Presumably in attempts to avoid confusion, it has since also been called Black Acacia, Black Locust and Yellow Locust.

Although known in Britain as early as 1640, the tree became forgotten and, when William Cobbett returned from America in 1819 extolling its virtues so enthusiastically, he sold over a million trees from his Kensington nursery and people thought of it as a novelty. Many of Cobbett's million trees no doubt still exist, for the tree is relatively common today, but they have certainly not ousted the oak as he forecasted.

The False Acacia is now to be found in many temperate parts of the globe but is grown commercially mostly in Italy and Korea, where it has a reputation for soil improvement and the prevention of soil erosion.

False Acacia grows to a height of 80 feet and develops a deeply furrowed, dark grey bark. The alternate, pinnate leaves, from 6 to 12 inches long, have from five to eleven pairs with one at the tip. The pendulous racemes of fragrant, white, pea-like blossom in early summer are reminiscent of the Laburnum. The branches are brittle but the timber is remarkably durable in contact with the soil and therefore useful for gateposts, fence posts and such purposes.

False Acacia, *Robinia pseudoacacia*, with leaves, flowers and bean-like fruit

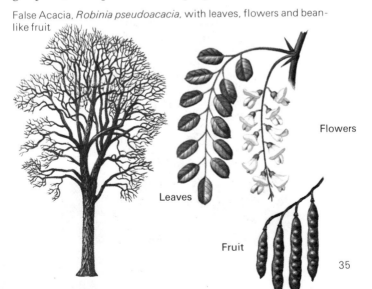

Flowers

Leaves

Fruit

White Salee, *Eucalyptus pauciflora,* is a hardier species of eucalyptus, which can survive snow and grow at higher altitudes. One characteristic is its picturesquely twisting trunk. (*Below*) the Cider Gum, *Eucalyptus gunnii,* the hardiest species of eucalyptus grown in Britain

Gum (Eucalyptus)

To think of gum trees is almost to think of Australia. For many visitors to that country the first impression is the odour of eucalyptus wafting on the breeze. There are over 500 species in this genus and perhaps more awaiting discovery. They are evergreen, some are shrubs, some tall trees and most of them natives of Australia or Tasmania.

Gum trees are a special feature of the Australian landscape. The only part of this immense land where the climate will support tree growth is a coastal strip seldom more than 100 miles wide. Thirty-eight per cent of that area is afforested, a proportion very considerably greater than either world or European averages, and in those forests ninety-four per cent of all the trees are eucalypts.

In Britain few eucalypts will survive the winter cold and then only in the more favoured parts. They are widely grown, however, in the Mediterranean countries, Florida and California, South America and South Africa.

The name gum arises from these trees' habit of exuding gum from the trunk. The botanical name *Eucalyptus* means 'well covered' and refers to the cap or calyx, which covers the stamens until they open, when it falls off. The beauty of the flowers lies in the stamens, usually yellow or red.

The leaves are quite entire and a distinctive feature in most species is that the juvenile leaves are quite different from the adult ones, the former being opposite, heart-shaped and without stalks. When the tree becomes adult and reaches the flowering stage, the leaves are then alternate, stalked, longer and more pointed.

Another curious characteristic, not easy to see without a magnifying glass, is a margin or vein, sometimes pink in colour, which runs round the edge of the leaf. The leaves are usually quite hairless, bluish-green in colour. The bark is very prone to peel off, sometimes falling away in tube-like pieces. Although some eucalypts can exceed 300 feet, the seeds of even these giants are remarkably small.

The aromatic and antiseptic eucalyptus oil, once so popular in the treatment and prevention of common colds, is obtained by the distillation of leaves. In Australia the timber trees are not used for this purpose but rather the 'mallee', as the dwarf, multi-stemmed shrubby eucalypts are called, which grow in the drier inland areas.

Of the many species of gum, a few of the more common are:

Bloodwood (*Eucalyptus corymbosa*) is a tree of medium size with persistent bark.

Blue Gum (*E. globulus*), which reaches 200 feet in its native Tasmania and Victoria, and around 100 feet in warmer south-western parts of Britain. Is the most widely planted gum in North America and has boomerang-shaped leaves.

Cider Gum (*E. gunnii*) is not highly regarded in its native Tasmania or South Australia (where it will reach 100 feet) but it appears to be the hardiest species in England.

Ironbark is the name given to several eucalypts: *E. crebra,* Narrow-leaved Ironbark; *E. fergusoni,* Grey Ironbark; *E. leucoxylon,* White Ironbark; *E. paniculata,* also known as Grey Ironbark; *E. siderophloia,* Broad-leaved Ironbark, and *E. sideroxylon,* the Red Ironbark. This group is of economic importance in Australia for its extremely hard timber.

Jarra (*E. marginata*) is grown commercially in south-western Australia. Its rich red and hard, very durable timber is often known as Western Australian mahogany and is the most widely known of all Australian woods throughout the world. It grows to 150 feet.

Karri (*E. diversicolor*) of Western Australia grows to 200 feet, producing the second best-known Australian timber closely resembling Jarra. If a sliver of wood is burned, the ash will be white if it is Karri, black if it is Jarra.

Mountain Ash (*E. amygdalina regnans*) is a variety of the Peppermint Gum, and is the tallest of all the eucalypts. Early explorers credited it with heights of 500 feet but a reward offered in 1888 failed to produce a tree higher than 326 feet. The timber, together with that of *E. obliqua,* is often marketed as Tasmanian oak. The bark of the latter peels off in large pieces and was used for aboriginal canoes.

The Red or Scarlet-flowering Gum (*E. ficifolia*) is a striking tree with scarlet stamens and dark red anthers making individual flowers 2 inches across in corymbs 7 inches wide.

The Spotted Gum (*E. maculata*) loses its bark in patches and grows to 150 feet. It has a variety which is lemon-scented (*Eucalyptus citriodora*).

Tasmanian Snow Gum (*E. cocei-fera*) grows up to the tree-line on the island mountains. In exposed places it is often stunted, but in more favourable places it can attain a height of 70 feet.

The Ghost Gum, *Eucalyptus papuana* is a native of the island of New Guinea and North Australia. Its name alludes to its almost white bark

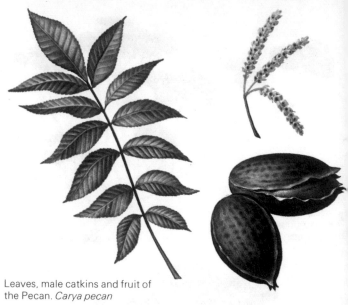

Leaves, male catkins and fruit of
the Pecan. *Carya pecan*

Hickory (Carya)

These are deciduous trees with alternate, pinnate leaves.
Closely allied to the walnuts, they are distinguished by the
husks of their nuts splitting into four, while those of the
walnut split into two.

Most of the hickories are natives to the eastern United
States. *Carya* belongs to a group of genera (*Decumaria,
Liriodendron, Nyssa, Sassafras* and *Symphoricarpos* are the
others) originally thought to be solely native to eastern North
America – until species were found in eastern Asia.

Hickory is grown commercially in south-eastern Canada
and the central eastern United States for its timber which,
being springy, tough and yet light, is used for tool handles,
sports goods and the other purposes for which ash is employed
in Britain. The nuts are often edible but one species, the
Pecan, is grown specially for this purpose.

In spite of their attractive foliage, which turns a lovely
yellow in autumn, hickories are not often seen in gardens and
parks because they resent the root disturbance normal nursery routine involves.

Hornbeam (Carpinus)

The Common Hornbeam (*Carpinus betulus*) is the tallest of its genus (up to 80 feet) and native to Britain, Europe and Asia Minor. Sometimes mistaken for beech, its leaves are rougher and its trunk becomes fluted with age. It is often planted as a hedge to provide wind shelter because, when clipped in summer, it holds its leaves through winter.

The hardness of the timber is recognized in its name and it makes durable flooring and mechanical parts such as the action of pianos. It can be dyed black to resemble ebony and is sometimes used in inlay-work. It burns brightly and hornbeam torches were used by the Ancient Romans at weddings.

Other species come from various temperate parts of the northern hemisphere. The American Hornbeam (*C. caroliniana*), also known as Blue Beech, grows only to 40 feet and has sharply pointed leaves, 2 to 4 inches long and often doubly toothed, which turn a deeper yellow, or even a beautiful scarlet in the autumn.

Common Hornbeam, *Carpinus betulus*, (*left*) and American Hornbeam or Blue Beech, *Carpinus caroliniana*, (*right*)

Seed

Catkin

Catkin

Horse Chestnut (Aesculus hippocastanum)

The common Horse Chestnut is neither a chestnut nor a favoured food of horses. The sweet chestnuts we eat are from quite another tree (see page 30). The nuts inside their spiky conkers ('conquerors') certainly look like chestnuts but, while not poisonous, they are too bitter for human food and, although cattle, deer and sheep all apparently enjoy them, horses do not. One theory is that for many years before they were introduced to the West they had been a popular medicine in Persia for broken-winded horses; another is that the name refers to the horseshoe-like mark left on the bark of young branches at the point where a leaf has fallen.

The original home of the Horse Chestnut was long disputed. Northern India was suggested and forests are still to be found in west Pakistan and the central Himalayas. However, it is now generally agreed that they are natives of northern Greece and Albania. Seed came to Vienna in 1576 and the trees are now found across Europe and in North America.

In the golden age of the English stately home, avenues of these handsome trees were planted, one of the best known

(*Opposite*) avenue of Horse Chestnuts. *Aesculus hippocastanum*, and detail of flower and leaf (*top left*). (*Top right*) flower of the red Horse Chestnut, *Aesculus x carnea* and (*immediately above*) a 'conker' the fruit in its prickly shell. (*Right*) leaves and flowers of Lignum Vitae, *Guaiacum officinale*

being that at Bushey Park, where General Eisenhower had his headquarters before D-day in World War II.

There is a red-flowered form of Horse Chestnut (*A. carnea*) which is probably a natural hybrid between *A. hippocastanum* and *A. pavia*, the Red Buckeye, a native of North America.

Lignum Vitae (Guaiacum officinale)

This evergreen tree is indigenous to tropical America and the West Indies, about 15 to 30 feet high, with smooth, variegated, white and green bark. The timber is hard, heavy and unsplittable and used for rollers and bowling 'woods'. The wood was brought to Europe by Spaniards early in the sixteenth century and in a decade achieved a reputation as a remedy for syphilis – hence its name, 'wood of life'.

43

Lime, linden or basswood (Tilia)

The tall, pyramid-shaped, handsome lime or linden tree with
its yellowish-white sweetly fragrant blossom so beloved of
the bees is a familiar part of the European scene, planted in
streets, such as Berlin's famous 'Unter den Linden', along
canal banks in the Netherlands and as avenues leading to the
splendid mansions of the past.

The old or European name of linden is commemorated in
such place names as Lyndhurst in the New Forest and the
newer name of lime in the Limehouse district of London's
East End (limehouse being derived from limehurst, which
means a wood of limes).

The Common Lime (*Tilia europaea*), which is most frequently seen, is a hybrid. Its parents are believed to have been
the Small-leaved Lime (*T. cordata*) and the Large-leaved Lime
(*T. platyphylos*). Many thousands from Holland were planted
in England during the seventeenth century, 4,000 being
imported in 1662 for Hampton Court.

The Small-leaved Lime grows to 80 to 90 feet, has leaves from $1\frac{1}{2}$ to 3 inches long that are dark green and hairless on the top surface and pale with tufts of red-brown hairs in the vein axils. This is the last of the three to flower.

The Common Lime grows to 100 to 130 feet, has larger leaves of $2\frac{1}{2}$ to 4 inches, with paler hairs beneath. It flowers soon after mid-summer. The Large-leaved Lime also grows to 130 feet and has 2 to 5 inch leaves that are dark green and hairy on both sides, densely so beneath. The twigs are downy and its fruits are larger. It flowers first in mid-summer.

The American Lime (*T. americana*) grows to 130 feet in its native land and has very long leaves of up to 8 inches, 3 to 6 inches wide.

The fibrous inner bark of the European limes is used for mat-making and Russian peasants make shoes from it. The old-fashioned garden tying material 'bass' or 'bast' came from this source. In America lime trees are often known as basswood. The lime tree is not related to the tree which gives us lime juice (see *Citrus*, page 112).

Locust
(See False Acacia, page 34)

(*Opposite*) an avenue of lime trees, *Tilia*, on the banks of a canal in Delft. (*Below*) the leaves, flowers and fruit of the Common Lime, *Tilia europaea*

The Mahogany Tree, *Swietenia macrophylla* or *mahogani*, (*below*) with detail of the leaves and flower (*above*) and the fruit (*left*)

Mahogany (Swietenia)

For centuries mahogany has been one of the most popular of all woods for cabinet making. Its colour is pink when freshly cut but it darkens with seasoning and dyes are often used to achieve the 'mahogany colour'.

The Mahogany Tree (*Swietenia macrophylla* or *S. mahogani*) is a broad-leaved evergreen of the American tropics. The latter species, *S. mahogani*, is grown in the West Indies and southern Florida, where it reaches a height of some 75 feet. The leaves are up to a foot long and these trees are sometimes planted in streets for shade.

Most of the timber used for furniture comes from *S. macrophylla*, a 100-foot tree of the tropical rain forests of Venezuela, Colombia, Ecuador, and the upper reaches of southern tributaries of the Amazon. Vast tracts of this forest have still to be used.

Apart from the real mahogany, timber of more or less similar colour, grain and figure from a number of other trees is sold under such descriptions as African Mahogany(*Khaya*), Australian White Mahogany (*Eucalyptus*), Gaboon Mahogany (*Aucoumea klaineana*), etc.

Mangrove (Rhizophora)

Few trees will withstand salt water and no tree can survive with its roots permanently submerged, thus cutting off its oxygen supply. Yet the Mangrove (*Rhizophora*) is able to flourish in salt water tidal swamps, doing this by producing aerial roots, some as thick as a man's arm, which spread out from the trunk in a dense tangle of growth, rooting their tips into the mud.

The American Mangrove (*R. mangle*) grows in shallow swamps where the land is under water at high tide, along the coast of Florida and the Atlantic coast of central America. Other species of mangrove grow in similar conditions in tropical Africa, India and the Philippines.

The swampy nature of the ground and the tangled aerial roots make such forests almost impenetrable yet the timber of mangrove, being durable, is used for such purposes as piling and posts, while the bark, rich in tannin, is in demand locally for leather tanning.

American Mangrove,
Rhizophora mangle

Maple (Acer)

The maples belong to a large genus, with many species from all temperate parts of the northern hemisphere. Most are deciduous, a few are shrubby and some evergreen.

The typical maple leaf is palmate with five lobes, but some species have only three lobes, others thirteen. There is one group with no lobes and another, the *negundo* group, in which the leaves are compound pinnate with three, five or seven leaflets. In all cases the leaves are opposite. Their fruits consist of a pair of sections joined at their base and known as 'keys'. Each key contains a seed and a flat membrane, or wing, which ensures wide dispersal of the seed.

The Common Maple (*Acer campestre*) is a native of Europe but is relatively uncommon in England. It is a round-headed tree, seldom exceeding 30 feet in England, and is often less where it occurs in hedgerows and has been subjected to lopping.

(*From top to bottom*) Common Maple, *Acer campestre;* Montpelier Maple, *Acer monspessulanum;* Black Maple, *Acer nigrum;* Italian Maple, *Acer opalus*

This species has often been used for topiary work and ornamental hedges, the 50 feet high hedges at Schönbrunn, near Vienna, being a notable example. It is also known as the Field Maple or Hedge Maple.

The Norway Maple (*A. platanoides*) is common throughout Europe. Other beautiful European species are the Montpelier Maple (*A. monspessulanum*) and the Italian Maple (*A. opalus*).

The Box Elder (*A. negundo*) is a native of North America but has been grown in England since 1688. Also from North America are the Red, Scarlet or Swamp Maple (*A. rubrum*), which grows to 120 feet and has red flowers, the Black Maple (*A. nigrum*) with its black, deeply-furrowed bark, the Silver Maple (*A. saccharinum*) with smooth, grey bark, and the Sugar Maple (*A. saccharum*) which yields maple sugar and syrup.

From a number of Japanese species stems a hoard of varieties popular in gardens and parks for their autumn tints (see also Sycamore, p. 66).

(*From top to bottom*) Norway Maple, *Acer platanoides;* Red Maple, *Acer rubrum;* Silver Maple, *Acer saccharinum;* Sugar Maple, *Acer saccharum*

Common Oak,
Quercus robur

Oak (Quercus)

The oak has constantly recurred in the pattern of British history. It played a part in the ancient ceremonies of the Druids, the forming of the New Forest by decree of William the Conqueror in 1079, the death there of his son, Rufus, the building of a navy which won an empire, the supply of charcoal for gunpowder. For centuries the oak has supplied Britons with the timber for their everyday needs, their furniture, domestic utensils and support for the roof over

Leaves and acorns of the Common Oak. The leaves are on very short stalks, even stalkless, while the acorns are on long stalks

their head. Is it any wonder that the oak is still the most familiar of trees in Britain today?

In actual fact there are two distinct species native to Britain, the Common Oak (*Quercus robur*) and the Durmast Oak (*Q. petraea*), both of which grow wild right across Europe from Ireland to Asia Minor. The Common Oak bears its leaves on very short stalks or on none at all, and its acorns singly or in bunches of several on stalks up to 5 inches long. The leaves of the Durmast Oak, on the other hand, have definite stalks about an inch long while the acorns are stalkless or clustered quite close to the twigs.

These distinctions appear clear enough but in practice it will be found that many oaks exhibit intermediary characteristics and there are many hybrids. A considerable number of varieties, too, have been recognized of which the Cypress Oak (*Q. robur fastigiata*), a slim tree with erect branches, the Weeping Oak (*Q.r. pendula*), the Fern-leaved Oak (*Q.r. asplenifolia*) and the Durmast variety called *mespilifolia*, with medlar-like leaves, are examples.

The theory has been advanced that the Durmast Oak is the true English Oak and that the Common Oak, *Quercus robur*,

Leaves and acorns of the other species of oak common to Britain, the Durmast Oak, *Quercus petraea*. The leaves of this oak have definite stalks, while the acorns are almost, or quite, stalkless.

51

Burr Oak,
Quercus macrocarpa

Chestnut-leaved Oak,
Quercus castaneifolia

Common Oak,
Quercus robur

Cork Oak, *Quercus suber*

Kermes Oak,
Quercus coccifera

Holm Oak,
Quercus ilex

was a foreigner, introduced from overseas. For a number of reasons this seems difficult to believe.

Today the Durmast Oak seems to prefer the stonier soils of the west and north, while the Common Oak flourishes better on the deeper soils of southern England but there is evidence that the Common Oak was once more abundant everywhere. One notes, for instance, the curious survival of the Common Oaks of Wistman's Wood, growing on Dartmoor in conditions more likely to be congenial to Durmast Oaks.

The Common Oak produces acorns at an earlier age and in greater quantity than the Durmast. At one time oak trees were valuable as a source of pig food and in the Domesday Book some oak woods were valued by the number of pigs they would support. The Common Oak would, therefore, have been grown in preference to the Durmast. Moreover, the branches of the Durmast tend to be straighter and the crooked branches of the Common Oak were the more useful to form the 'crucks' of houses and the curved timbers of ships.

A final confirmation of this can be seen in the oak leaves and acorns carved on the roof bosses and beneath the misericords in the oldest churches – acorns with stalks, and oak leaves without, typical of *Quercus robur*.

The word *quercus* is simply the old Latin word for oak and *robur* means strength, referring to the timber. Durmast appears to be derived from 'derw', the Celtic word for oak and 'mast' meaning the acorns. *Petraea* refers to this species' liking for rocky soil, while the word acorn, the fruit or corn of the oak, derives from the old English word ac, for oak. The famous horse race, the Oaks, which takes place at Epsom three days after the Derby, was named in 1779 after an estate belonging to its founder, the Earl of Derby.

The Common Oak has been widely planted in the temperate parts of the globe. There is, for instance, a famous mile-long avenue of these oaks at Twyford, Hastings in New Zealand, but the native habitat of the oak is mostly confined to the northern hemisphere. Height, habit and leaf-shape in particular differ considerably between the many species but all bear their nut-like fruits in 'egg-cups' although here again there are some marked differences in detail.

From Japan, Korea and China came the Daimyo Oak

(*Q. dentata*) remarkable for its foot-long leaves and *Quercus variabilis* with its acorns almost enclosed by the curly scales of its cup. From the Caucasus and Persia came the Chestnut-leaved Oak (*Q. castaneifolia*) with its leaves resembling those of the Sweet Chestnut and its acorns lodged in shaggy cups. This oak should not be confused with the Chestnut Oak (*Q. prinus*) of North America, also called the Rocky Oak because it grows on dry, rocky soils.

The Kermes Oak (*Q. coccifera*) is quite a small tree, native of southern Europe, north Africa and Asia Minor. It is the host of an insect related to the cochineal which, in mediaeval times, was used to make a scarlet dye.

The Cork Oak (*Q. suber*), the prime source of commercial cork, comes from southern Europe and Africa, and is one of several evergreen oaks. The Holm Oak (*Q. ilex*), native of the Mediterranean regions but growing on the Scilly Isle of Tresco, is another, resembling the Holm or Holly Tree.

Other well-known European species include the Portuguese Oak (*Q. lusitanica*) which is semi-evergreen in southern Europe, the Pyrenean Oak (*Q. pyrenaica*) notable for its deeply indented leaves and ovoid acorns often borne in pairs, and the Turkey Oak (*Q. cerris*) from southern Europe and Asia Minor which grows quickly and up to 120 feet high.

North America has some sixty species of oak in some of which the leaves turn a beautiful red colour in autumn. Examples of these are the Northern Red Oak (*Q. borealis*) and its taller variety *Q. borealis maxima,* the Pin Oak (*Q. palustris*) and the Scarlet Oak (*Q. coccinea*).

Other outstanding American oaks include the Burr Oak (*Q. macrocarpa*) otherwise known as the Mossy-cup Oak because of the whiskers on its acorn cup, the White Oak (*Q. alba*), the Spanish or Southern Red Oak (*Q. falcata*) which is American in spite of its name and is not notable for its autumn leaf colouring, and the Willow Oak (*Q. phellos*) with

(*Opposite*) 1. Pin Oak, *Quercus palustris;* 2. Portuguese Oak, *Quercus lusitanica;* 3. Northern Red Oak, *Quercus borealis maxima;* 4. Pyrenean Oak, *Quercus pyrenaica;* 5. Scarlet Oak, *Quercus coccinea;* 6. Spanish or Southern Red Oak, *Quercus falcata;* 7. Lucombe Oak, *Quercus x hispanica lucombeana;* 8. White Oak, *Quercus alba;* 9. Willow Oak, *Quercus phellos*

Pepper Tree or
Peruvian Mastic
Tree, *Schinus
molle*, with example
of leaf and berry-
like fruit

leaves which seem much more typical of a willow than an oak.

The number of cultivated hybrids and varieties is legion. Some of the best-known hybrids are Bartram's Oak (*Q. x heterophylla*) discovered about 1812 growing in a field near Philadelphia belonging to a John Bartram, the Lucombe Oak (*Q. x hispanica lucombeana*) raised accidentally in 1765 in the Exeter nursery of a firm called Lucombe and Pince, and Turner's Oak (*Q. x turneri*) raised about 1750 in Spencer Turner's nursery at Holloway Down, Essex.

To the uninitiated, oak-apples appear as small nut-like excrescences, like some kind of seed vessel, a variation of the acorn. In fact they are caused by tiny wasps which pierce a twig and lay their eggs within. The tree makes extra tissue to cover these foreign bodies and so the gall develops. When the eggs hatch the larvae then eat their way into the open. The host tree is apparently little harmed by the shelter it thus provides and in Asia Minor a species of oak (*Q. infectoria*) particularly liable to attack is specially grown and the galls or oak-apples are collected, and from them are extracted tannin and gallic acid.

Pepper Tree (Schinus molle)

The Pepper Tree is a native of South America but is planted as a street tree in southern Europe, South Africa and the Antipodes, and has been widely planted as an ornamental in California and Florida where it is now wild.

It is evergreen, growing from 20 to 50 feet with graceful drooping branches. The rosy-red fruits are the size of small peas. It is also known as the Peruvian Mastic Tree because of the resinous mastic it yields.

Persimmon (Diospyros)

Two species of *Diospyros* are grown for their fruits; *D. kaki*, a native of Japan and China and *D. virginiana*, a native of North America. The former is grown for ornament as well as for its fruit in Australia and the latter is common in the South Atlantic and Gulf States of the United States and its timber is used for textile shuttles and the heads of golf clubs.

D. ebenum of Ceylon and India is the source of the black wood we know as ebony, used for the black keys of pianos. Ebony also comes from other species of *Diospyros* grown in Africa.

(*Above*) leaves and fruit of Persimmon, *Diospyros virginiana*, and (*below*) the leaves and fruit of the tree that produces the black wood known as ebony, *Diospyros ebenum*

Plane trees in The Mall, London, England. This species, the London Plane, is a hybrid, *Platanus x acerifolia*.

Plane (Platanus)

If ever there were a case for the wider use of Latin names, it lies here. *Platanus* known in England as the Plane, is called Sycamore in North America. In England the name Sycamore is applied to *Acer pseudoplatanus*, which the Americans call the Sycamore Maple and the Scots call the Plane. The word 'sycamore' means fig-mulberry and therefore is only properly applied to the mulberry-like fig tree from Egypt and Syria, *Ficus sycamorus*.

The leaves of *Platanus* have a certain resemblance to those of the maples but whereas the latter are in pairs, the Plane leaves are alternate. A characteristic feature of the Planes is their spherical seed vessels, sometimes known as button-balls. These are occasionally borne singly but more often anything from two to six hang from a drooping stalk. One sphere consists of many separate seeds each provided with a minia- ture 'parachute' of hairs. For some 1800 years physicians have accused these hairs, and also those of the leaves, of causing throat and lung irritation but apparently without affecting the popularity of the trees.

Buttonwood or the American Sycamore (*Platanus occidentalis*) grows to a height of up to 170 feet in its native southern and eastern United States and, although it experiences far more severe cold in Massachusetts, it is killed by spring frosts in Britain.

The Oriental Plane (*P. orientalis*) is a native of southeastern Europe and western Asia. It is a very long-lived tree and there are tales of trees that are still living, beneath which the Crusaders rested, or even Hippocrates sheltered 2,300 years before.

The London Plane (*P. acerifolia*) is believed to be a hybrid between *P. occidentalis* and *P. orientalis* but when or where they met, nobody knows. Perhaps it was in Spain where the first trees from the New World were brought.

London Planes flourish along stream banks, as do other species, yet are remarkable for succeeding when planted in the pavements of smoky city streets. Their habit of casting their bark in large flakes may help them to withstand the grime.

Leaves and fruit of the Oriental Plane, *Platanus orientalis*

Poplar or cottonwood (Populus)

Apart from the Aspen (see page 22) there are over thirty species of poplar, widely grown over the temperate parts of the northern hemisphere, and so many hybrids and varieties that their identification is difficult even for the expert.

In North America they are known as cottonwoods, a reference to the white, cottony down which surrounds the seeds and ensures their wide distribution in the wind. In gardens this spring 'snow storm' can be quite unpleasant and one of the worst offenders can be the Eastern Cottonwood (*Populus deltoides* also called *P. monolifera*) a native of the eastern United States. In fact, poplars are not good trees for garden surroundings: they litter the ground with catkins in spring, uncommonly slippery leaves in autumn and many small twigs whenever there is a gale. Still worse, their roots may block drains, lift road or path surfaces and, particularly in clay soils, even upset the foundations of nearby buildings.

Lombardy Poplar,
Populus nigra italica

Poplars are nearly always dioecious and have two characteristics in common with willows, to which they are related: they flourish in damp soil and they will root readily from cuttings. Many a fence post of poplar has grown to make a tree.

Another characteristic of all poplars is their rapid growth and one of the fastest is the Black Cottonwood or Western Balsam Poplar (*P. trichocarpa*) of the west coast of North America. These are said to reach 200 feet in their native land, but much less in Europe. A specimen at Kew reached 55 feet in 13 years.

In Europe the best-known poplar name is probably the Lombardy Poplar (*P. nigra italica*). To many people its mention immediately conjures pictures of tree-lined roads and rivers in France. It is fastigiate, and grows to 100 feet or more, often forming a striking landmark. Its bark is deeply grooved with slightly spiral furrows.

The origin of the Lombardy Poplar is obscure and it seems to have had no more connection with Italy than that the first specimen in England was imported from Turin by Lord Rochford in 1758. These first trees were

(*Above*) leaf and catkins of the Black Poplar, *Populus nigra,* and (*below*) leaf and catkins of the Eastern Cottonwood, *Populus deltoides*

61

all males, as are most in England today, being propagated from cuttings. A few rare females exist from later importations.

The Black Poplar (*P. nigra*) is native to Britain, Europe and western Asia. Various reasons have been suggested for its name; that a dark circle is seen at the middle of the trunk when a tree is felled, that its bark is dark and, the most likely, that its leaves are darker than those of the White Poplar (*P. alba*). The Black Poplar and the Eastern Cottonwood of America are the parents of the Black Italian Poplar. A variety of this hybrid (*P. x serotina erecta*) is commonly grown in northern Italy. Like the Lombardy Poplar it is of columnar growth, but a little more spreading.

The White Poplar or Abele (*P. alba*) is a native of central and eastern Europe and western Asia, now widely grown in the United States. It has a smooth grey bark and the young leaves have a white felt on their lower side which falls during summer. The timber of this tree was used for making soldiers' shields because it would take a blow without splitting, a quality which later commended its use for the bottoms of barrows and carts, and the making of packing cases.

The Grey Poplar (*P. canescens*) is very similar to the White and they are often confused. The Grey tree has ovate leaves on its leading shoots, not palmate, grey rather than white on the under side. In the south of England the Grey Poplar is more common than the White.

With a pleasing balsam-like fragrance in spring is the poplar known as Balm of Gilead or Ontario Poplar (*P. gileadensis,* previously known as *P. candicans*). This tree is often mistakenly called the Balsam Poplar (*P. tacamahaca,* previously known as *P. balsamifera*) which it closely resembles, although it is more spreading, has broader leaves and downy leaf-stalks and young shoots. Both have a great tendency to sucker, both scent the air in spring.

(*Opposite*) Balm of Gilead or Ontario Poplar, *Populus gileadensis,* formerly known as *Populus candicans.* (*Right top*) Leaves and catkins of the White Poplar, *Populus alba,* and (*below*) leaves and catkins of the Grey Poplar, *Populus canescens*

Male

Female

Male

Female

Leaves, flowers and fruit of the Service Tree, *Sorbus domestica*

Sandalwood (Santalum album)

A native of the East Indies, this evergreen derives its name from its Persian name, *Shandal*. It is also grown in Australia where there are some native santalums. The timber is sold as 'sandalwood' and is characterized by a distinctive perfume, for which reason it is used for lining cabinets, making joss-sticks and Chinese funeral 'furniture'. It yields an aromatic oil used for perfumes and medicinal purposes.

Sassafras

This is a genus of three deciduous species. *Sassafras albidum* is native to North America where the bark and roots used to be boiled to make Sassafras tea, once a popular spring tonic. Chips of the wood are used in the dyeing industry. The other two species belong to China and Formosa.

Service Tree (Sorbus domestica)

The Service Tree is native to western Asia, southern Europe and north Africa and has been grown in Britain since very early times. It seems probable that the name 'Service' was once applied to all species of Sorbus and that 'Service' (once spelled 'Servis' and 'Sorvis') is a corruption of *Sorbus*, the Latin name for the fruit used by Cato and Pliny. A related species, the Mountain Ash (*Sorbus aucuparia*) has been called the Birdcatcher's Service, a reference to the use of its berries for baiting traps.

The fruit of *Sorbus domestica* is either pear- or apple-shaped, about an inch long, and can be eaten when bletted, or partially decayed, like medlars. The Service Tree is long-lived, probably five or six hundred years. A tree in Wyre Forest, Worcestershire, England, was thought to be old in 1678. It lived until 1862 when it was set on fire by a tramp.

Sorbus domestica is sometimes called the True Service Tree to differentiate it from the Wild Service (*S. torminalis*) native to Britain. A much more common *Sorbus* is the Whitebeam (*S. aria*), which flourishes on chalky land.

(*Above*) leaves and flowers of the Sassafras, *Sassafras albidum* and (*below*) leaves and fruit of the Whitebeam, *Sorbus aria*

Silk-Cotton Tree (Ceiba casearia or pentandra)

Widely grown in the tropics this tall deciduous tree reaches a height of 120 feet. The cotton-like fibre which protects its seeds forms commercial kapok. The fragrant flowers are showy and the tree is sometimes planted to provide shade.

Silky Oak (Grevillea robusta)

The Silky Oak is the tallest member of a genus of trees and shrubs all natives of Australia, Tasmania and New Caledonia. In its homeland it can grow to 150 feet but in America and Europe it is sometimes grown from seed as an indoor pot plant. It is also grown as a shade tree for coffee and tea plantations in Africa, India and Ceylon, and as an ornamental tree in the United States. Another tree of the same family is also called the Silky Oak (*Cardwellia sublimis*). This is common in the brush forests of north Queensland supplying timber exported as Australian Silky Oak.

The Strychnine Tree, *Strychnos nux-vomica*, provides a poison, curare, for South American hunters' poisoned darts and arrows

Leaves, flowers and winged
seed vessels or 'keys' of the
Sycamore, *Acer pseudoplatanus*

Strychnine Tree (Strychnos nux-vomica)

The Strychnine Tree belongs to a genus of tropical trees and
shrubs many of which possess virulent properties. This one is
the source of strychnine and its timber, known as Snake-
wood, has a bitter taste which saves it from termite attack.
Curare, the South American arrow poison, first brought to
Europe by Sir Walter Raleigh in 1595, and Akazga, the West
African ordeal poison, were both compounded from extracts
of *Strychnos* species.

Sycamore (Acer pseudoplatanus)

Known as the Plane in Scotland and the Sycamore Maple in
America, the Sycamore (*Acer pseudoplatanus*) is the largest
hardwood tree native to Europe and western Asia. Although
not a native of Britain it has been naturalized for several
centuries and grows so easily that it is often regarded rather
in the nature of a weed, its characteristic wind-borne keys
(see under Maple, page 48) ensuring the appearance of seedlings in the most inappropriate places. It is a hardy tree, perhaps thriving better in Scotland and the north of England than
in the south, and withstands salty coastal winds.

In spite of its Latin name, there is only a certain superficial
likeness to the Plane tree in the colour and shape of the leaves.
Those of the Sycamore are, however, opposite while the
Plane's are alternate. The leaves are attacked by a parasitical
fungus (*Rhytisma acerinum*) which causes the small black
patches frequently noticed when the leaves fall.

Teak (Tectona grandis)

Teak trees are indigenous to India, Burma, Thailand, Vietnam and Indonesia, and are of great economic importance for the wood is remarkably durable and strong, yet easily worked and of moderate weight.

The trees will reach a height of up to 150 feet. The Indian specimens may branch at 15 feet but in Burma a 90 foot length of clean bole is not unknown. Elephants are still widely used to carry the logs from the forest to the nearest river or railway. When the rivers are used, as happens in Burma, it may take five years from felling until the log reaches Bangkok —and a loss of twenty-five per cent has to be allowed for on account of thefts in transit.

Tulip tree (Liriodendron)

There are two Tulip Trees – the Chinese (*Liriodendron chinense*) and the American (*L. tulipifera*). The former is shorter, up to 50 feet, with smaller flowers; the latter grows to 200 feet near the Appalachian Mountains and 100 feet in Britain where it is the more common.

Elephants carrying logs of Teak, *Tectona grandis,* in a Burmese forest

Liriodendron belongs to the same botanical family as the Magnolia which is often mistakenly called the Tulip Tree because of its prominent tulip-like flowers. The true Tulip Tree does have flowers which are reminiscent of tulips of the lily-flowered type but they are less showy in colour and, high up on a large tree, less noticeable, and therefore in Britain (and the Antipodes) these trees are grown more for their attractive and unusual foliage and stately proportions than for their decorative blossom.

The Chinese species was first noted growing in the Lushan Mountains in 1875 and the American species was brought to England some time prior to 1688 when Bishop Compton had a specimen at Fulham Palace. By 1745 a tree at Waltham Abbey had reached a height of 96 feet.

In America this tree is sometimes known as Yellow Poplar and its timber as American Whitewood. It is widely used there for plywood. Exported to Britain the timber is sometimes called Canary wood. At one time it was in demand by cabinet-makers. It is easily worked and made a good lining material for furniture drawers.

Flowers, fruit and leaves of the American Tulip Tree, *Liriodendron tulipifera*

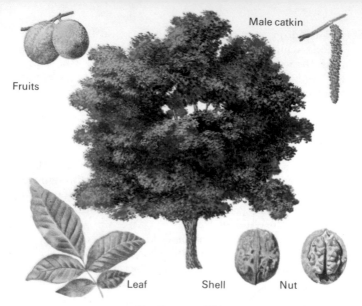

Fruits

Male catkin

Leaf   Shell   Nut

The Common Walnut, *Juglans regia*

Walnut (Juglans)

Originating in eastern Europe and Asia, the Common Walnut (*Juglans regia*) has long been grown in southern Europe and England. It was highly regarded by the Romans who named it *Juglans* which is a corruption of *Jovis glans,* meaning the nuts of Jove or Jupiter, and Linnaeus emphasized its special status by naming it *regia*. The word walnut derives from the old English *wealh knutu,* meaning the 'foreign nut'.

When it was first grown in England, the walnut was most prized for its nuts which provided food, oil for burning, cooking or medicinal use and the husks were useful as a stain or dye. Later, the timber was much used for making furniture and the stocks of guns. It is a curious fact that although walnut timber has been valued for some 500 years supply has never equalled demand and it still enjoys a special status as much for its rarity as for its undoubted beauty.

Although Common Walnut is grown in North America, where it may be called English or Persian Walnut, there are several native species – *Juglans californica* (the Californian

Walnut), *J. cinerea* (Butternut), *J. hindsii*, *J. major* and *J. nigra* (Black Walnut) are best-known.

China has a special variety of *J. regia* and Manchuria and Japan their own species. Such a valuable timber has its imitators. Among these are the so-called East Indian Walnut (*Albizzia lebbek*) popularly called Woman's Tongue Tree because the rustling leaves are never silent, and the Walnut Bean (*Endiandra palmerstonii*) of northern Queensland, a Laurel, which gives decorative 'Australian Walnut' veneers.

West Indian Locust (Hymenaea courbaril)

Growing to a height of 60 feet, this evergreen is common in tropical America. Its reddish-brown wood is used locally as timber for building, furniture-making and ship-building, while it is of economic importance for its resin which is commercial copal, used in varnish-making.

(*From top to bottom*) Fruit, leaf and nut of the Black Walnut, *Juglans nigra;* the Butternut, *Juglans cinerea;* the Arizona Walnut, *Juglans major;* and leaf of *Albizzia lebbek,* the so-called East Indian Walnut or Woman's Tongue Tree

71

Willow or osier (Salix)

Willows grow throughout the cooler parts of the northern hemisphere. There are more than 250 species of deciduous trees or shrubs in this genus and identification is made difficult by the existence of numerous hybrids exhibiting intermediary characters. For instance there are at least 17 species native to Britain but each of these has hybridized with some of the others, even as many as nine. Furthermore, most willows have the sexes on separate plants, but not invariably so, and, when they do, the male and female trees sometimes

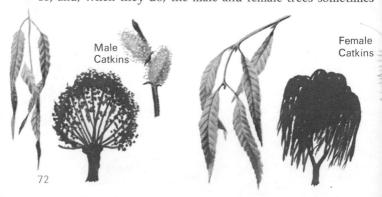

Male Catkins

Female Catkins

exhibit other differences than merely possessing either female flowers or male catkins.

Most willows prefer a damp situation and such species are widely planted along river banks to prevent erosion and to make use of wet land where little else would flourish. The trees are often pollarded and assume grotesque shapes which give no idea of their beauty when grown naturally.

The Weeping Willow (*Salix babylonica*) was first introduced to western Europe from Asia Minor and it was assumed that this must be the willow 'by the rivers of Babylon' on which the Jews hung their harps, as recorded in Psalm 137. It is now thought that it originated in China. Curiously, the famous Willow Pattern, which depicts a willow unknown to botanists, was first evolved in England and later copied by Chinese potters.

The Cricket Bat Willow (*S. coerulea*) is also known as the Blue Willow because its leaves have a bluish tinge. Its origin is unknown and is thought by some to be a variety of the White Willow (*S. alba*) which has a markedly silvery appearance, young shoots and the lower sides of the leaves being covered with a silky down. Another theory is that it is a hybrid between *S. alba* and the Crack Willow (*S. fragilis*) which derives its name from the tendency for its supple branches to break off from the trunk.

Left to its own devices the Cricket Bat Willow can reach a height of 100 feet but, when grown in the eastern counties of England for cricket bats, it is felled as soon as a diameter of 18 inches has been acquired. The Common Osier (*S. viminalis*) is widely grown near water for basket-making.

Male Catkins

(*Above opposite*) pollarded White Willows, *Salix alba,* growing along a river bank in England. This is not the tree from which cricket bats are made. (*Across the bottom from left to right*) leaves, silhouette of tree and catkin of the Common Osier, *Salix viminalis;* the Weeping Willow, *Salix babylonica;* the Pussy Willow, *Salix discolor*

FOREST TREES – CONIFERS
Cedar (Cedrus)

The Cedars are majestic trees indeed, most of them tall, all of them with widely-spreading branches. They make a conical shape in their earlier years and then, having reached their full height, the branches extend outwards and the tree assumes a more flat-topped appearance. They develop an immense girth which probably accounts for over-estimations of the age of individual specimens. All carry upright, barrel-shaped cones and stiff, needle-like leaves borne in tufts on the short spurs and arranged spirally on the leading branches.

Four species are usually recognized but they are so alike that some botanists argue they are only geographic variations of the same species. The four are the Atlas Cedar (*Cedrus atlantica*) from the Atlas Mountains of north Africa, the Cedar of Lebanon (*C. libani*) from the Lebanon and Taurus Mountains, the Cyprus Cedar (*C. brevifolia*) from Cyprus and the Deodar or Indian Cedar (*C. deodara*) from the western Himalayas.

The Cyprus Cedar grows only to 40 feet, bearing the

smallest cones. The Atlas Cedar has cones up to 3 inches long; Cedar of Lebanon, 3 to 4½ inches; Deodar, 3 to 5 inches. In their native habitats the Cedar of Lebanon grows to 100 feet, the Atlas Cedar to 120 feet and the Deodar to 200 feet.

A simple way of memorizing differences between the three taller species is: 'A for ascending, L for level, D for drooping'. The branches of the Atlas Cedar tend to ascend, those of the Lebanon Cedar are nearly level, while those of the Deodar tend to droop.

The Cedars of Lebanon were hewed by the servants of Hiram for Solomon's temple. Today these trees are dying out in their native land and only small islands of trees remain. Gone, too, are the great forests of north Africa which supplied ancient Rome with its cedar, although the Atlas Cedar is still grown commercially in Morocco and Algeria. Only in the Himalayas do the largest of all the cedars still reign in their ancient majesty.

(*Opposite*) the majestic Cedar of Lebanon, *Cedrus libani*. (*Below left*) the Atlas Cedar, *Cedrus atlantica*, with ascending branches and detail of cone and leaves, (*right*) the Deodar or Indian Cedar, *Cedrus deodara*, with drooping branches and (*centre*) the cedar of Lebanon, *Cedrus libani*, with level branches

75

Fir (Abies)

Ancient Greek and Roman writers considered the words 'fir' and 'pine' as interchangeable and, until the last century, 'fir' usually meant any conifer. Even later, botanists were not agreed as to whether a fir and a spruce belonged to the same genus, so the popular names often lead to confusion. Now it is generally recognized that the pines belong to the genus *Pinus,* the spruces to *Picea* and the true firs to *Abies.*

Nearly all the pines have long needle-like adult leaves borne in tufts of two or more (pages 80 to 83). The leaves of the true fir (*Abies*) grow singly, direct from the branch and if you pull one off, it will come away cleanly leaving a distinct, round scar on the twig, whereas a spruce leaf will tear away with a little strip of bark. The cones of Hemlocks, Douglas Firs and Spruce (pages 86 and 87) all hang downwards; those of the true firs stand upright.

(*From top to bottom*) cone of Silver Fir, *Abies alba;* Balsam Fir, *Abies balsamea;* Colorado White Fir, *Abies concolor.* Cones of all true firs stand upright and when they fall they disintegrate on the twig leaving the core like a miniature flagpole on the twig.

(*Left*) cone of Douglas Fir, *Pseudotsuga menziesii,* (*right*) Eastern Hemlock, *Tsuga canadensis* (*top*), and Western Hemlock, *Tsuga heterophylla.* (*Centre*) flagstaff in the Royal Botanic Gardens, Kew, England. It is made from a Douglas Fir, 225 feet high and is in one piece. The tree was about 370 years old and before shaping weighed 39 tons.

Douglas Fir (Pseudotsuga menziesii, formerly taxifolia)

The Douglas Fir is an important timber tree in North America where it grows in vast forests and in Britain millions a year are now being planted. It has grown to 400 feet in British Columbia; time has yet to decide what it can reach in Britain.

Its Latin name commemorates its discovery in 1797 by Dr Archibald Menzies, RN, while its popular name perpetuates that of David Douglas who first obtained seeds.

Hemlock (Tsuga)

The hemlock spruces are evergreens from North America and the Orient. The cones hang down from the tips of branches or twigs. Eastern Hemlock (*Tsuga canadensis*) and Western Hemlock (*T. heterophylla*) are native to North America where they are grown for their timber. Western Hemlock is now being planted in Britain.

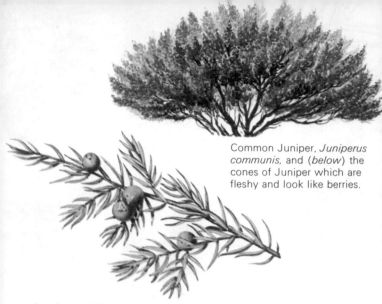

Common Juniper, *Juniperus communis,* and (*below*) the cones of Juniper which are fleshy and look like berries.

Juniper (Juniperus)

This is a genus of evergreen trees and shrubs, occurring widely in temperate and sub-tropical regions of the northern hemisphere. One species (*Juniperus communis*) is native to Britain and may be found on chalk hills.

The fruits are more berry-like than cone-like. The Common Juniper (*J. communis*) has dark purple, globular 'berries' that are fleshy when ripe. Although not true berries, the term 'Juniper berries' is often used. The word 'gin' is a contraction of 'juniper', the berries providing the flavour.

An African (*J. procera*) and American species (*J. virginiana*) are known as the African and American Pencil Cedar. Their timber is easily whittled and is used for making pencils.

Kauri pine (Agathis)

This genus of evergreen conifers are renowned for their symmetry and bronzy-green foliage. Young trees shed their lower branches and the branchless trunk is remarkably free of knots. The species *Agathis australis* is from North Island, New Zealand. Its important timber-producing forests have now been decimated by uncontrolled logging.

Larch (Larix)

The Larch is one of the few deciduous conifers. In youth they are of pyramidal shape but become more spreading with age. In spring as the leaves and red female flowers appear on the Common Larch (*Larix decidua*) it appears very graceful.

The Common Larch is a native of central and northern Europe, and Russia and Siberia. It was introduced to Britain about 1629 but regarded as an ornamental until the Duke of Atholl planted 873 larches at Blair Atholl and another 350 at Dunkeld between 1740 and 1750. They prospered and between 1816 and 1826 the then Duke planted nearly 10 million. Other landowners followed suit and the Larch became, economically, the most important forest tree in Britain.

The Japanese Larch (*L. leptolepis*) with bluish-green foliage came to Britain in 1861 and, planted alongside the Common Larch at Dunkeld, produced hybrid seedlings (*L. x eurolepis*) which grow faster than either of their parents.

(*Below*) the Common or European Larch, *Larix decidua* (*left*) with detail of the cone and two of its varieties *Larix decidua pendula* (*centre*) and *Larix decidua fastigiata* (*right*)

Scots Pine,
Pinus sylvestris

Pine (Pinus)

There are more pines growing in the northern hemisphere than any other tree and the approximately seventy species come from all the northern temperate regions, occasionally from the warmer parts and sometimes found as far north as the Arctic Circle and beyond. Some species will survive conditions which one might think would inhibit all plant growth, in places where a few feet down the soil is permanently frozen and where the surface, around the roots, thaws out only long enough to permit a growing season of six to eight weeks.

It is as a quick-growing source of softwood that pines are grown in such vast numbers and in addition to their native northern hemisphere they are now being planted by the million in South Africa, Australia and New Zealand.

One species alone, the Monterey Pine (*Pinus radiata*, formerly *P. insignis*), is of no great economic importance in its native California but it grows so rapidly in the Antipodes that it now constitutes over half the coniferous forests of Australia and is the predominant species in the New Zealand forests, claimed to be the largest man-planted forests in the world.

In the latter country, Monterey Pine is sometimes ready for felling in 30 years, nearly always in about 50 years.

Pines are evergreen, very resinous and some grow up to 200 feet. In one species alone (*P. cembroides monophylla*) the leaves are borne singly, in most other species in clusters of from two to five, and in a few cases clusters of six. The adult leaves are thin, narrow and needle-like, often finely toothed and they always have on at least one surface rows of tiny whitish dots, called stomata.

Where leaves are in pairs it will be found that together they make up a cylinder, so that the individual leaves are semi-circular in section. Where there are three or more leaves, they will form a cylinder when held together and each leaf is triangular in section.

Male and female flowers appear on the same tree, the former as short yellow or reddish catkins, the latter as reddish embryo cone-like growths at or near the tips of the year's

(*Left*) Monterey Pine, *Pinus radiata*, with leaves and cone and (*below*) cone and leaves of *Pinus cembroides monophylla*, the only pine species to bear single leaves

growth. The cones take two seasons to develop, sometimes longer, may be borne singly, in pairs or in clusters. They vary considerably in shape and size from species to species.

The Scots Pine (*P. sylvestris*) is the only conifer native to Britain of economic importance for its timber although very few of the original wild trees are still growing today. In modern times it has been extensively planted and about a seventh of the total forest area of Britain is now devoted to this one species. The Forestry Commission still plants many millions annually, but it is now planting even more of the Lodgepole Pine (*P. contorta*) from British Columbia and Alaska, the pine used by the Red Indians to support their lodges.

Growing on their own, or in small clumps, mature Scots Pines can be picturesque, especially when the low rays of the setting sun find a reflection in the red tints of the bark and the branches form blue-green, asymmetrical patterns against the

The Lodgepole Pine, *Pinus contorta*, which has leaves in pairs, was used by Red Indians as a framework for their wigwams or lodges.

(*Above from left to right*) cones of Armand's Pine, *Pinus armandi;* Bishop Pine, *Pinus muricata;* Maritime or Cluster Pine, *Pinus pinaster.* (*Left*) Austrian Pine, *Pinus nigra*

sky. They are not, however, exclusive to Scotland and are native to most of Europe and as far as Siberia.

Some pines have edible seeds. Among such are the Mexican Nut Pines or Pinyons (*P. cembroides* and varieties), the Swiss Stone Pine (*P. cembra*) of central Europe, Russia and Siberia, and the Stone Pine (*P. pinea*) of Mediterranean regions.

The Weymouth Pine (*P. strobus*) was introduced to Britain from eastern North America in the eighteenth century and planted extensively by Lord Weymouth but it is not planted now because of attacks by a fungus and an aphid.

(*Below from left to right*) Mountain Pine, *Pinus mugo;* Jack Pine, *Pinus banksiana;* Northern Pitch Pine, *Pinus rigida;* Western White Pine, *Pinus monticola;* Weymouth Pine, *Pinus strobus*

Podocarpus

This genus of more than sixty species of evergreen trees and shrubs originates mostly in the warm regions of the southern hemisphere. Some species are grown in the southern United States for ornamental purposes and in sheltered districts of Ireland and Cornwall. In many species the stalk of the rather plum-like fruit is brightly coloured, fleshy and edible.

Several species are grown in South Africa under the name of Yellow Wood. At heights of over 100 feet they are South Africa's tallest tree. New Zealand White Pine (*Podocarpus dacrydioides*) grows to 150 feet and is a useful timber tree. *Podocarpus koreanus,* resembles the Irish Yew, and grows in the warmer parts of Australia.

Redwood (Sequoia sempervirens)

The Redwoods of Oregon and California are the tallest trees in the world and among the oldest. The name Sequoia derives from Sequoyah, a Cherokee Indian leader.

In southern, sheltered parts of Britain they grow rapidly and have exceeded 100 feet. In their native land the highest recorded was 340

Leaves of *Podocarpus nagi,* from Japan

Leaves and cone of the Redwood, *Sequoia sempervirens*

feet. It comes as something of a surprise to find that such a majestic giant bears such small cones – up to 1 inch long. The evergreen leaves are rather yew-like and the reddish-brown bark may be nearly a foot thick.

When a Redwood is felled it will often send up new growth from dormant buds near the base, an unusual feature for conifers. At one time the Redwood and the Wellingtonia (page 88) were regarded by botanists as belonging to the same genus. Today these two species are the only survivors of some 40 species which grew in prehistoric forests.

Rimu (Dacrydium cupressinum)

This is a cypress-like tree, really more akin to the Yew and the *Podocarpus*. Rimu is native to New Zealand where the timber is used for railway sleepers, furniture and building. Another species, the Huon Pine (*D. franklinii*), has slender, pendulous branches, and comes from Tasmania.

(*Left*) comparison in size of the Redwood with Nelson's Column, England and the Statue of Liberty, New York. (*Right*) a forest of Redwoods, the tallest trees in the world

(*Right*) Norway Spruce, *Picea abies*

(*Above*) West Himalayan Spruce, *Picea smithiana*

(*Left*) Serbian Spruce, *Picea omorika*

Sitka Spruce, *Picea sitchensis*

Spruce (Picea)

The shape and general appearance of the Common Spruce (*Picea abies,* formerly *excelsa*), sometimes known also as the Norway Spruce or the Spruce Fir, may well be familiar to more people than that of any other tree for, in its nursery stage, this is the most popular conifer for a Christmas tree. Its pyramidal shape is characteristic, although when grown close to other trees it soon loses its lower branches. The branches radiate in tiers and the short, glossy-green, needle-like leaves are arranged spirally on the shoots.

Pulling off a growing Spruce leaf will take with it a piece of bark, but when the leaf falls naturally it leaves a tiny stump on the twig. These little stumps on the shoots provide one more means of distinguishing the Spruce from the fir (*Abies*). The cones are usually pendulous, those of the Common Spruce being cylindrical and 4 to 6 inches long.

Now one of the best-known forest trees in Britain, it was re-introduced some time before 1548. It is a native of nearly all Europe, except Denmark and Holland, and geological excavations have shown that in fact Spruce grew in Britain when the upper strata of the Tertiary period were laid down. In Britain the Common Spruce only grows to 100 to 120 feet but in the Carpathians it will reach as high as 200 feet.

Spruces may be divided into two groups. In one group, to which Common Spruce belongs, the leaves are foursided and have stomata on each surface. In the other group the leaves are flat in cross-section and have stomata only on the back surface of the leaf which usually twists so that this surface is on the underneath side.

In this second group will be found the Sitka Spruce (*P. sitchensis*), a native of the north-western coastal regions of North America. Although introduced from Canada in 1831, Sitka Spruce was not planted in Britain in any numbers until after World War I: now it is one of the United Kingdom's most important conifers, being planted throughout Wales and down the west side of England and Scotland.

(*Top*) the Norway Spruce, *Picea abies*, and (*below*) a tiny Norway Spruce, the most popular conifer for use as a Christmas Tree

Wellingtonia (Sequoiadendron giganteum)

Formerly included in the same genus as the Redwood (*Sequoia*), the Wellingtonia is not such a tall tree but a giant nevertheless. The General Sherman Tree in Sequoia National Park is 272 feet tall, but there have been specimens exceeding 300 feet. The age of the tallest trees has been a matter of argument among experts, some estimating as much as 4,000 years, some only 1,500: the few remaining very tall specimens are now protected trees.

The reddish-brown bark of the Wellingtonia is very thick, up to 2 feet in the tallest trees, and resistant to fire, an attribute which must have been an important factor in enabling these trees to survive for so many centuries.

The Wellingtonia is also known as the Big Tree, the Mammoth Tree and, in America, the Giant Sequoia. Its popular name, however, was at one time the subject of fierce nationalism. The tree was first found on the western slopes of the Sierra

A famous Wellingtonia, *Sequoiadendron giganteum*, the General Sherman Tree in Sequoia National Park, United States. It is over 270 feet tall.

Nevada, California, in 1841 by General John Bidwell and seed was taken to England in 1853. The discovery of this 'new' forest giant aroused tremendous interest and it was named after Britain's most famous citizen, the Duke of Wellington. The Americans retaliated by naming it *Washingtoniana*, which did not 'stick' in the same way as Wellingtonia in England.

Yew (Taxus)

Because it clips easily, one is apt to think of the yew as a hedge shrub rather than the 40-foot tree it really is. Before the invention of gunpowder the timber was valuable for making bows and at one time was popular for furniture. Yew is still used for decorative veneers, for turning and for fence or gate posts as it is resistant to damp.

Yews are widely distributed over northern temperate regions. There are several species, although some authorities hold that these are merely geographical varieties of the Common Yew (*Taxus baccata*). The seeds, leaves and branches are poisonous and when the leaves wither, their toxicity increases, so clippings should never be left on the ground.

Common Yew, *Taxus baccata;* tree (*above*) and leaves and fruit (*below*)

89

GARDEN AND PARK TREES – BROAD-LEAVED

Acacia (Mimosa)

The feathery foliage and yellow globular flowers of Mimosa (*Acacia dealbata*) are an attractive sight in florists, but it is the powerful fragrance which makes Mimosa so popular. Spring-time branches come from the French Riviera but this Silver Wattle will grow outdoors near the English south coast (see also Acacia, page 18).

Almond (Prunus communis or amygdalus)

The wild Almond is grown in many temperate parts of the globe for its beautiful single pink or white flowers produced early in spring. There are many varieties, some with double pink flowers. A popular one is *pollardii,* an Australian-raised hybrid of an almond and a peach. It has large, slightly fragrant, pink flowers deepening to crimson at the centre.

Bottle tree (Sterculia or Brachychiton)

Sterculia is a genus of some 250 deciduous and evergreen trees of tropical Asia, South America, Africa and Australia. The

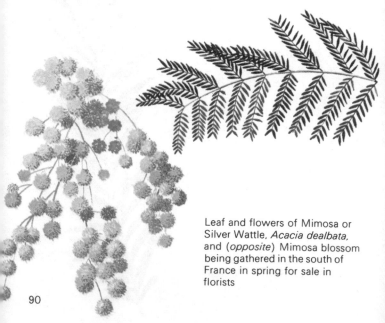

Leaf and flowers of Mimosa or Silver Wattle, *Acacia dealbata,* and (*opposite*) Mimosa blossom being gathered in the south of France in spring for sale in florists

name *Sterculia* derives from *stercus* meaning dung and refers to the unpleasant odour of the flowers of some species. The name Bottle Tree is very appropriate for the Queensland representative of the genus, *Sterculia rupestris,* a semi-deciduous species which grows up to 50 feet in height but has a bottle-shaped trunk which may have a girth of 35 feet.

The Illawarra Flame Tree (*S. acerfolia*) from New South Wales and Queensland is a favourite ornamental in Australia. The bright scarlet calyxes of the flowers, borne in foot-long panicles, give this tree its name and when every branch blooms at the same time, a 100-foot tree makes a remarkable sight. Another popular Australian species is the Kurrajong (*S. diversifolia*) on which no two leaves are the same.

Cape Chestnut (Calodendron capense)

This ornamental evergreen tree of South Africa grows to 60 or 70 feet in height and bears panicles of bloom, white or pinkish in colour, 4 or 5 inches across and somewhat more in length. It was introduced to Britain in 1789 but needs the warmth of a heated greenhouse. It is planted outdoors in south Florida. Sometimes grown in New Zealand, it is more popular in Australia where the climate suits it better.

Indian Bean Tree, *Catalpa bignonioides*, with details of the leaves, flowers and bean-like seed pods

Catalpa

When the species *Catalpa bignonioides,* the Indian Bean Tree, was introduced to Britain in 1726 this was thought to be a genus entirely of the New World. Its name, Catalpa, is an American Indian one. Since those days several species have been found in China and Japan.

Catalpas are popular lawn and park trees, hardy in Britain and the United States. The panicles of trumpet-shaped flowers, white, yellowish-white or pale purple, sometimes with yellow markings and purple spots, can be very showy.

A hybrid (*C. x hybrida*), a cross between *C. bignonioides* and *C. ovata* from China, is much planted in the central United States. In Britain *C. bignonioides* is more popular. A feature of the Catalpas are the seed pods, 12 inches or more long, looking remarkably like French beans.

Cherry (Prunus)

Many varieties of flowering cherry are grown in gardens for the sake of their flowers. Most originated in Japan, the land of cherry blossom, and make trees from 5 to 40 feet tall. There are also weeping species which are very decorative in the garden. One such is *Prunus avium pendula* and another is *P. subhirtella pendula,* the Weeping Rosebud Cherry.

Crab apple (Malus)

Many species of wild or crab apple are to be found in various parts of the north temperate zone and a vast number of crosses and varieties are produced for garden use. Not only the blossom, which is often sweetly scented, but also the little fruits, are highly decorative.

Malus pumila is the Wild Crab Apple of Britain, Europe and western Asia, and an original parent of orchard trees. The apples are much smaller than dessert kinds, and very sour, but some of them make an agreeable jelly. Varieties grown in Britain include 'Dartmouth', 'John Downie', and 'Wisley Crab'.

The European Wild Crab was taken across the Atlantic by early settlers and is now naturalized there. True native American crabs include the Southern Crab (*Malus angustifolia*) with apples an inch across, the Sweet Crab Apple (*M. coronaria*) which in spite of its name bears sour, inch-wide fruit, the Biltmore Crab (*M. glabrata*) with triangular-shaped leaves, and the Prairie Crab Apple (*M. ioensis*) with fruit an inch long but which is much smaller in diameter.

Crab Apple, *Malus pumila*, with some of the fruits from the many varieties

Dogwood (Cornus)

The dogwoods, also known as cornels, are shrubs and small trees, popular in gardens for their pretty bracts in spring and their red or yellow shoots in winter. Most species are deciduous and natives of North America.

A favourite species is *Cornus florida,* the Flowering Dogwood, growing up to 20 feet in Britain and to 40 feet in the States. It has white, occasionally, pink, petal-like bracts, scarlet fruits and the leaves turn scarlet in autumn.

Flowering Dogwood, *Cornus florida,* (*above*) and (*below*) May or Hawthorn, *Crataegus monogyna*

Hawthorn or may (Crataegus)

In Britain this small tree flowers in May or early June and is held by some to be the explanation of the warning proverb 'Cast ne'er a clout till May be out'. If the weather is settled fine and warm, the hawthorn blossoms the sooner of course.

There are two common British and European native species – *Crataegus oxyacantha* (15 to 20 feet) and *C. monogyna* (up to 35 feet) and a wealth of cultivated varieties. One is *C. monogyna praecox,* the Glastonbury Thorn, which flowers in winter and is said to be descended from St Joseph of

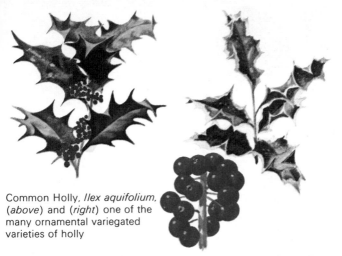

Common Holly, *Ilex aquifolium,* (*above*) and (*right*) one of the many ornamental variegated varieties of holly

Arimathea's staff which, when struck into the ground near Glastonbury in the first century AD took root and flowered on Christmas Day.

Several hundred species of thorn are native to North America. The thorns have red, black, yellow, blue or plum-coloured fruits, known as haws, are deciduous and nearly all of them are spiny.

Holly (Ilex)

As is the case also with hawthorns, holly is often so severely pruned in gardens to keep it within the bounds of a hedge or, in the case of holly, to provide Christmas 'greenery', one is apt to forget it can become a tree.

There are some 300 species of holly coming from temperate and tropical regions all over the globe, the western side of North America and Australia and New Zealand being exceptions. Some are deciduous but the evergreen species are most favoured for garden planting.

Ilex aquifolium is the Common Holly of Britain, Europe, north Africa and western Asia, and there are many varieties, some with green leaves, others with gold or silver variegations. The American Holly (*I. opaca*) is very similar, growing to 50 feet, but having larger leaves and fewer berries, technically 'drupes'.

Leaves and flowers of the Judas Tree, *Cercis siliquastrum, (left)* and leaves and fruit of Liquidambar, *Liquidambar styraciflua, (above)*

Judas Tree (Cercis siliquastrum)

This tree grows to 40 feet and the pea-shaped flowers appear in the spring before the leaves. Of oriental origin, it was supposed to have been the tree from which Judas Iscariot hanged himself. American species are the Eastern Redbud (*Cercis canadensis*) and Californian Redbud (*C. occidentalis*).

Laburnum

The laburnums are festooned all over with racemes of clear yellow in spring. They are natives of southern Europe and western Asia, the so-called Scotch Laburnum (*Laburnum alpinum*) having been brought from southern Europe in about 1596. *Laburnum alpinum pendulum,* with weeping branches, is a particularly lovely variety. The Common Laburnum (*L. anagyroides*) is sometimes called the Golden Chain Tree.

Laurel (Prunus)

Two more members of the *Prunus* genus are the Common or Cherry Laurel (*Prunus laurocerasus*) and the Portugal Laurel

(*P. lusitanica*). They will make attractive trees of 20 feet or more but all too often are severely pruned and become shrubby. They are evergreens, the leaves of the Portugal Laurel being darker and smaller.

Lilac (Syringa)

This is a very popular flowering tree, or shrub, in both English and American gardens. Most garden varieties have been raised from the Common Lilac (*Syringa vulgaris*) brought from eastern Europe in the sixteenth century. The name 'Syringa' is frequently, but mistakenly, applied to the Mock Orange (*Philadelphus*).

Liquidambar

Liquidambar comes from the Latin *liquidus*, a liquid, and *ambar*, amber, and refers to the sweet-smelling resin obtained from the inner bark of *L. orientalis* once used in the preparation of friar's balsam. The American species, *L. styraciflua*, is known as the Sweet Gum and has some resemblance to the Maples (*Acer*) but the leaves are alternate, not opposite. This is the most common species in Britain and Australia but only grows to 80 feet in Britain, compared with up to 140 feet in its native land.

Common Laburnum or Golden Chain Tree, *Laburnum anagyroides*, (*left*) and the Common Lilac, *Syringa vulgaris* (*right*)

Magnolia

The magnolias are natives of North and central America and eastern Asia. They are mostly deciduous, with fragrant flowers some of which, individually, are the largest of any tree's. The most widely grown magnolia is *Magnolia x soulangeana*, a hybrid between two Chinese species, *M. liliflora* and *M. denudata*, of which there are many varieties.

As with its parent *M. denudata*, the flowers of *M. soulangeana* begin to open before the leaves appear and they may be up to 6 inches across. Even larger are the creamy-white, fragrant blooms of the American species, the Southern Magnolia (*M. grandiflora*), which may be 10 inches across.

(*Above*) *Magnolia x soulangeana*. The flowers appear before the leaves and the colour is dependent on the variety. (*Below*) *Prunus cerasifera atropurpurea*, formerly well-known as *Prunus pissardii*

Mountain Ash or Rowan (Sorbus aucuparia)

This is a favourite tree for British gardens and parks for the autumn colouring of its leaves and its clusters of bright red 'berries' (strictly, pomes), which do not remain long as they are most attractive to birds. *Sorbus aucuparia* may grow to 60 feet and be too large for the average garden, but there are a number of varieties which are less vigorous and not so suitable.

It is native to Britain, Europe and western Asia, but now widely planted in North America. The American Mountain Ash (*S. americana*) has longer leaflets, grows to 30 feet and is more widely planted in Australia than the European.

Peach (Prunus persica)

Ancestor of our peaches and nectarines grown for their delicious fruits, the original wild Peach is also often grown in gardens for the sake of its pale rose blossom in spring. Some varieties have double flowers of white, pink or even deep red.

Plum (Prunus)

Last, of the *Prunus* fruit family grown for decoration are the flowering plums. The Cherry or Myrobalan Plum (*P. cerasifera*) originated in western Asia but is often found in hedges in Britain. A favoured variety is *atropurpurea* (formerly, *pissardii*) with blush-pink buds opening to white, and ruby-red leaves gradually darkening to wine colour, finally purple. It was found in Persia by the Shah's gardener, M. Pissard.

Leaf, flower and fruit of the Mountain Ash or Rowan, *Sorbus aucuparia*

Queen Crape Myrtle (Lagerstroemia)

Two deciduous species of *Lagerstroemia* sometimes find a place in gardens and parks in the warmer countries. These are the Queen Crape Myrtle (*L. speciosa*), 60 feet or more high with mauve to purple flowers up to 3 inches across, and the ordinary, hardier Crape Myrtle (*L. indica*), growing only up to 20 feet and with smaller, white, pink or red flowers.

Crape Myrtle is native to China and grows well in Australia and Italy. It only flowers in the warmest parts of Britain. The name Crape refers to the crinkled petals of the flowers.

Spindle Tree (Euonymus europaeus)

The Spindle Tree, from Europe is a deciduous tree up to 25 feet high, with attractive pinkish-red, berry-like fruits. There is a variety with white fruits (*albus*), one with pink fruit (*aldenhamensis*) and one with purple leaves (*purpureus*).

The evergreen *Euonymus japonicus* is sometimes planted as a windbreak, as, for instance, round the bulb fields of the Isles of Scilly, and when clipped becomes shrubby.

There are some 120 species of *Euonymus* but many are shrubs rather than trees. *E. atropurpureus* from the eastern United States, is called the Wahoo or Burning Bush. It sometimes grows to 25 feet with purple flowers and crimson fruits.

Strawberry Tree (Arbutus unedo)

Superficially, the fruits of this evergreen tree bear a remarkable resemblance to strawberries while the white flowers in short panicles are very like Lily-of-the-valley. A native of the Mediterranean countries and southwest Ireland, it reaches its finest development (20 to 40 feet) on the shores of the Lakes of Killarney. There is a variety with pink flowers (*rubra*), which was found growing wild near Glengariff, Cork.

Although the fruits can be eaten without harm, they are not exactly tasty and Pliny said the name *unedo* derived from the words *unus*, one, and *edo*; to eat, inferring that you might eat one, but never a second.

(*Opposite*) 1. Strawberry Tree, *Arbutus unedo;* 2. Leaves, flowers and fruit of the Strawberry Tree ; 3. Leaves and seed capsules of the Spindle Tree, *Euonymus europaeus;* 4. Leaves and seed capsules of the Wahoo or Burning Bush, *Euonymus atropurpureus*

(*Left and above*) Lawson's Cypress, *Chamaecyparis lawsoniana*, and (*right*) a compact columnar form of Lawson's Cypress, *Chamaecyparis lawsoniana allumii*

GARDEN AND PARK TREES – CONIFERS

Cypress

The evergreen trees commonly known as cypresses are divided by botanists into two genera, the true cypress (*Cupressus*) and the false cypress (*Chamaecyparis*). This distinction has only been made comparatively recently and species of false cypress are still often referred to as *Cupressus*.

The large cones of the true cypress produce from six to twenty seeds on each fertile scale and the seedlings have from two to five cotyledons. In both *Cupressus* and *Chamaecyparis* the juvenile leaves are soft and needle-shaped, and only $\frac{1}{3}$ inch or less in length. The adult leaves of the true cypress are on plump or angled branchlets while those of the false cypress have a flattened branch system. The smaller cones of the false cypress produce only one to five seeds per fertile scale and the seedlings only two cotyledons.

The cypresses are widely used for hedges and shelter, to provide a contrast and background to the bright colours of flowers and as specimens to give contrast and winter foliage in flower beds. Dwarf varieties are often planted in rock gardens to lend height to the miniature landscape and provide interest in the winter. When used as hedges they are often so cut and clipped that one tends to forget that they are really tall and beautiful trees.

Apart from the one species *Chamaecyparis formosensis* (from Formosa), the false cypresses are hardier than the true cypress and transplant better. They are, therefore, very much more common in Britain where the hardier species of cypress really flourish only in the warmest parts.

A popular *Chamaecyparis* in Britain is *C. lawsoniana*, Lawson's Cypress, which will reach 200 feet but is frequently clipped to make a hedge. There are many varieties including *C.l. allumii,* a compact columnar form.

The Nootka Cypress (*Chamaecyparis nootkatensis*), a handsome tree from the western States of North America, is one parent of a hybrid, *Cupressocyparis leylandii,* Britain's fastest growing conifer. The other parent is the widely-grown *Cupressus macrocarpa,* the Monterey Cypress which will grow to 70 feet and is much planted in seaside gardens.

(*Right*) Nootka Cypress or Alaska Cedar, *Chamaecyparis nootkatensis;* (*centre*) Monterey Cypress, *Cupressus macrocarpa;* (*left*) *Cupressocyparis leylandii*, a hybrid between the other two species

Fossil Tree (Metasequoia glyptostroboides)

The popular name of Fossil Tree, although apt, has led some people to the erroneous idea that it had been raised from fossil seeds which had lain dormant for thousands of years, an idea as fallacious as that of the viable mummy seeds supposed to have been found in the Pharaohs' tombs.

The *Metasequoia* were prehistoric trees known only as fossilized remains. Ten species had been identified in Asia, Europe and North America and until 1945 it was thought that the genus was extinct. Then a Chinese botanist discovered specimens of *M. glyptostroboides* growing in central China.

Seed was collected by the Arnold Arboretum of Harvard University and distributed in 1948. So far Fossil Trees have grown well in sheltered parts of Britain.

The Fossil Tree grows to a height of 100 feet in its native habitat. It is deciduous and, as an ornamental, highly decorative with its fresh green foliage in spring, turning to pink in autumn. The foliage resembles that of the Redwood (pages 84 and 85) but its linear needles are longer. In America the Fossil

Fossil Tree or Dawn Redwood, *Metasequoia glyptostroboides*, with detail of leaves (*below*)

Tree is sometimes known as the Dawn Redwood.

Maidenhair Tree (Ginkgo biloba)

The Maidenhair Tree is a last representative of a prehistoric race that was once widespread. It was introduced to Europe from Japan about 1730 but probably came from China. It is unknown wild anywhere and owes its survival to planting by Buddhist monks.

The Maidenhair Tree will grow to 100 feet and derives its name from the similarity of its leaves to the Maidenhair Fern. There is only one species of Ginkgo, but several varieties; including *fastigiata, pendula* with drooping branches and *variegata,* with yellow patches on the leaves.

This family of only one genus with only one species, is something of a curiosity. It is classified as a gymnosperm, yet the ovule has a rudimentary ovary. Fruits are seldom produced in England: the kernels are sweet and edible, covered with a yellow flesh which smells unpleasant.

(*Top*) Maidenhair Tree, *Ginkgo biloba,* and (*centre*) leaves and fruit. (*Right*) these trees owe their survival to their planting in Buddhist monasteries

Monkey Puzzle, *Araucaria araucana*, (*above*) with leaves and developing young cone. (*Below*) Norfolk Island Pine, *Araucaria excelsa*

Monkey Puzzle (Araucaria araucana)

In its native land of Chile the Monkey Puzzle, or Chile Pine, is grown for timber, but has been planted in Britain, the United States and the Antipodes as a lawn tree. It is evergreen with a dense covering of spikey leaves.

Norfolk Island Pine (Araucaria excelsa)

Coming from Norfolk Island, New Zealand, this handsome tree, growing up to 200 feet, is grown along coastal town promenades. It can withstand salt wind but little frost.

Swamp Cypress (Taxodium distichum)

The Swamp Cypress, also known as the Deciduous Cypress and, in America, Bald Cypress, is from the swamps of the south-eastern United States where its base may be submerged for a part of the year and its branches festooned with Spanish Moss. It was planted in Britain as early as 1640 by John Tradescant the younger, gardener to Charles I, and since his day has often been planted in parks on the edge of ponds.

It grows to 120 feet, is pyramidal in shape when young but spreads with age.

The leaves are pretty in spring and again in autumn when they turn a rich brown. The Swamp Cypress will grow in well-drained soil, but can survive waterlogged conditions by producing hollow 'knees', above the water-line, which take air to the submerged roots.

Thuja

Thuja, with six species from North America, China and Japan, is a genus of flat-leaved conifers. *Thuja occidentalis,* American Arbor-vitae or Northern White Cedar is a 50-foot tree from the north-eastern United States. Varieties are widely planted in England for decoration and garden hedging. *Thuja orientalis,* the Chinese Arbor-vitae, is a shorter tree and may be distinguished by its branches curving upwards. The scales of the cones are curiously hooked. There are two types, one pyramidal, the other making a more rounded tree.

Thuja plicata, Western Arbor-vitae or Western Red Cedar, is a tall tree from west-coast North America, reaching 200 feet there. Sometimes known as Giant Thuja, it was introduced to Britain in 1853 and some have been planted in Kielder Forest, Northumberland, a 70,000-acre forest begun in 1926.

(*Left*) Swamp Cypress, known in America as the Bald Cypress, *Taxodium distichum* and (*right*) American Arbor-vitae or Northern White Cedar, *Thuja occidentalis,* with detail of cone and leaves

FRUIT TREES

Apple (Malus)

The apple is an important fruit in nearly all the temperate regions of the world and it has adapted itself to wide variations in climate. Thus, in North America it grows in Canada and as far south as the Gulf of Mexico.

This adaptability has been achieved by a multiplicity of varieties, some of which are at their best in quite a restricted locality. The popular French Calville Blanche d'Hiver will not flourish in Britain, for example, while the old D'Arcy Spice seldom succeeds far from its native county of Essex. Man has

Blossom, leaves and fruit of a cultivated apple

cultivated apples for his own use for so many thousands of years that the countless crossings which must have occurred between natural forms are now a matter of conjecture rather than history. Indeed botanists still argue as to which are the natural species.

Linnaeus (1707–78), the 'father' of modern systematic botany, called the apple *Pyrus malus* but nowadays it forms a genus itself and the ancient Roman name of *Malus* is used and *Pyrus* kept for the pears.

Apples still grow wild in Europe and western Asia; extensively in southern Kirghizia in Russia. Cultivated apples are probably largely descended from *Malus pumila* the Wild Crab (see also page 93) of which there are many varieties. One

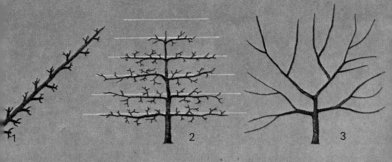

of these is *Malus paradisiaca,* the Paradise Apple, which is dwarf growing. Apples do not 'come true' from seed and named varieties are propagated by implanting a growth bud or graft on a rootstock of known vigour so that the subsequent size of the tree is predictable. The Paradise Apple is often used in this way to produce a dwarf tree.

The ability of the rootstock to affect the ultimate size of the tree has long been known. In the course of time many varieties of Paradise appeared, of varying performance, and they were given many names but also, with the course of time, they were frequently confused and given the wrong names.

Order was arrived at early this century, when the East Malling and Long Ashton Research Stations classified and defined the many rootstocks in use and propagated pure stocks of the best. Thus if an apple tree is bought today in Britain, America, or Australia, the nurseryman may say it is on, for instance, a Malling Type IX stock and we can be certain that it will never make more than quite a small tree.

Forms or shapes in which apples are grown in orchards or gardens ·
1. oblique cordon ; 2. espalier ; 3. bush ; 4. standard ; 5. pyramid ; 6 fan-trained

Apricot (Prunus armeniaca)

This golden-skinned stone fruit originated in China and came to Britain via the Middle East somewhere about 1500. In early gardening books it was referred to as the apricock, a transitional stage from the Arabic *al*, meaning 'the' and the Latin *praecox*, meaning 'ripening early'.

One of the best known varieties in England and in California is Moor Park which originated from a stone brought home in 1760 by Lord Anson, the Admiral who beat the French at the Battle of Cape Finisterre in 1747.

Flowering early in spring, the apricot is often harmed by late frosts and tends to be difficult to grow in England. In certain districts, however, it flourishes and one such is the village of Aynho, Northamptonshire, where a number of the cottages have apricot trees trained over the front walls.

The Japanese Apricot (*Prunus mume*) has some varieties cultivated for their fruit but more, including some with double flowers, are grown as ornamentals. Although much grown in Japan, this species also probably originated in China and Korea.

Apricot growing against the wall of a house in the village of Aynho, England, known as the 'apricot village'

Sir Francis Carew's trick to retard a cherry tree so that Queen Elizabeth I could enjoy the fruit a month after all other fruit had been picked

Cherry (Prunus)

Prunus avium, beloved by the birds (Latin *avis* means bird), is the ancestor of the sweet cherries, and *Prunus cerasus* gives sour ones, such as the Morello. There is also an intermediate type, known as Dukes, which can be cooked or eaten raw. These are probably hybrids between the two species.

Both *P. avium* and *P. cerasus* grow wild in Britain, yet Pliny recorded that having been introduced to Rome from Asia Minor about 70 BC, the Romans took them to Britain in the first century AD. Cherries were grown by the Saxons and in monastic gardens, and other varieties were brought by the Huguenots who established orchards in Norfolk and Kent.

When Queen Elizabeth visited Sir Francis Carew at Beddington she found that he had covered a cherry tree with a tent, kept continually wet, to retard the fruit so that she could enjoy cherries 'at least one moneth after all cherries had taken their farewell of England'.

An orange grove. (*Inset*) leaves and flower of the orange

Citrus fruits

The citrus group of trees flourishes in tropical and sub-tropical countries. Hardiest of all is the little kumquat from Hong Kong and China, with fruits only an inch or so in diameter. This has withstood temperatures as low as 12°F. The botanical name for kumquat is *Fortunella* but it is closely allied to *Citrus* and was formerly included in that genus.

Other citrus fruits are less hardy, orchard heating is resorted to even in California, and at the other end of the scale is the Lime (*Citrus aurantifolia*) which probably originated in India and southeast Asia, and will stand no frost. It is grown today in the West Indies and in the days of long sailing voyages was found to be a preventive of scurvy.

Next hardiest to the kumquat is the Calamondin (*C. mitis*) from the Philippines. Its $1\frac{1}{2}$ inch fruits have a deep orange flesh and are unsurpassed for making orangeade. It has recently acquired popularity as a house plant in Britain.

From Vietnam came the Tangerine or Mandarin (*C. nobilis deliciosa*) and the Satsuma (*C. nobilis unshiu*). The sweet orange most grown around the world is the 30-foot *Citrus sinensis,* also a native of Vietnam and China. There are many varieties and one, widely grown, is the Navel orange which is almost seedless and has a second, smaller fruit, enclosed within the larger one. The best marmalade is made from the fruit of the 30-foot Seville or bitter orange. (*C. aurantium*). Lemons (*C. limonia*) grow on small trees only 10 feet high. Common in Mediterranean countries, they came from Asia.

The Grapefruit or Pomelo (*C. paradisi*) is widely grown in the United States where it was introduced about 1809.

Oranges cannot be grown in the open in Britain and the first were introduced in the mid-sixteenth century before the invention of greenhouses. The trees were grown in tubs and taken into the shelter of sheds, heated by stoves, for the winter. Gradually these orangeries became quite ornate buildings. Old orangeries can still be seen at Hampton Court, Kensington Palace, Kew and in the grounds of many a stately home.

Citrus fruits : (*from top to bottom*) lemon, tangerine, orange, grapefruit

Ripe   Unripe

Date Palm (Phoenix dactylifera)

The palm family are monocotyledons while the other broad-leaved trees mentioned in this book are dicotyledons. They grow in the hot, drier parts of the world and have shiny-surfaced leaves, which do not easily lose moisture in the sun.

Of the many species of palm, the Date Palm is probably the most important, providing food, wine and sugar, and material for house roofs, hats, mats and so on. It probably originated in north Africa and Arabia, and is still one of the most common oasis trees. It is now widely cultivated.

Fig (Ficus carica)

The fig may have been brought to Britain from western Asia by the Romans but vanished until Cardinal Pole planted some at Lambeth Palace in 1525. A famous tree from Aleppo in 1648 is planted in a garden at Christ Church, Oxford.

Figs grown outdoors in England will develop their fruits without pollination and are seedless. In warmer countries fertilization, known as 'caprification', is achieved by a small wasp which transfers pollen from the trees bearing male flowers to those carrying the female flowers which are inside the embryo fruit. Only this wasp can creep down the tiny tunnel leading from the 'eye' of the fig.

There are over 600 species of *Ficus* growing in warmer countries. The Indian Banyan (*Ficus benghalensis*) is very large with a spreading top and the ability to send down aerial roots which, when established, produce fresh trunks. A single tree can eventually cover a large area. The Moreton Bay Fig or Australian Banyan (*F. macrophylla*), spreads 50 to 100 feet and is a familiar sight in Australian towns. The India-rubber Plant (*F. elastica*) grows to 100 feet in the wild but is also a popular house plant. When notched the stem produces caoutchouc but commercial rubber is from the Brazilian tree *Hevea*.

(*Opposite*) leaf, tree and fruit of the Fig, *Ficus carica*. (*Immediately below*) the Indian Banyan Tree, *Ficus benghalensis*, and (*across the bottom*) the Date Palm, *Phoenix dactylifera*; dates which form in great clusters; detail of flower; India-rubber Plant, *Ficus elastica*

Medlar (Mespilus germanica)

The Medlar grows wild in much of Europe but opinion is divided as to whether it is native to England. It is a spreading tree, hardly growing to 20 feet and the curious crooked growth of its branches gives it a picturesque appearance.

A taste for the fruit often has to be acquired. These are inch-wide, the shape of a flat apple but open at the end, and are stored until they almost rot, a process known as 'bletting', before they can be eaten raw.

Mulberry (Morus nigra)

The Common or Black Mulberry is a tree of picturesque appearance, up to 30 feet high, and bearing dark red oval berries, juicy and of agreeable flavour. Established trees can be propagated by rooting the tips of branches and it may be that some old trees have been enabled to survive by this means. In old trees branches often have to be supported.

A mulberry outside Canterbury was said to have been planted by Erasmus in 1516. Another, at Syon House,

Middlesex, was claimed to have been planted in 1548. As a food for silkworms, however, the leaves of the White Mulberry (*Morus alba*) are preferred. James I of England made vigorous attempts to promote a silk industry by importing mulberry trees and a thousand were sent to each county town.

Nuts (Corylus)

Some fifteen species of hazel nuts and filberts belong to the genus *Corylus* and grow in temperate parts of the northern hemisphere. In Britain the best-known types are the cobnut (*Corylus avellana*), with round nuts not quite covered by the husk, and the filbert (*C. maxima*), with long-shaped nuts completely covered by the husk. Perhaps the best-known variety of filbert has been misleadingly called 'Kentish Cob'.

A peculiarly twisted form of *C. avellana* (*C. a. contorta*) was discovered about 1863 in a Gloucestershire hedgerow. It is now nicknamed 'Harry Lauder's Walking Stick'. Natives to eastern North America are the American Hazel (*C. americana*) and the Beaked Hazel (*C. rostrata*).

All the above, however, are shrubs rather than trees but the Turkish Hazel (*C. colurna*) will make a tree of 80 feet while the Chinese Hazel (*C. chinensis*) will reach 120 feet.

Fruit and tree of the Common or Black Mulberry, *Morus nigra*

A Mediterranean olive grove with detail of the fruit and leaves of the Common Olive, *Olea europaea*

Olive (Olea europaea)

Probably originating in Greece and Asia Minor, the olive has been cultivated for its fruit in southern Europe since time immemorial. It is an evergreen tree, which grows slowly up to 40 feet and is much branched. The oil, squeezed from the $\frac{3}{4}$-inch oval fruits under pressure, is an important item in the diet of many Mediterranean people.

The olive will survive in Cornwall and against south-facing walls in southern England but it needs more warmth and sun than the wine grape to ripen its fruit. It is cultivated commercially in California and Arizona and is grown for ornamental purposes in other parts of the southern United States.

Apart from the Common Olive some fifty species of the genus *Olea* have been found in various parts of the eastern hemisphere, from the Himalayas to New Zealand. In Australia and New Zealand there is also a genus of many small trees and shrubs named Olearia (the Tree Aster or Daisy Tree) because of a resemblance of the leaves to those of the olive. An olive-branch has long been a symbol of peace.

Peach and Nectarine (Prunus persica)

Our English word 'peach' has derived, step by step, from *persica*, the Latin for 'Persian'. Persea, pesca, peshe, pesche, pêche were intervening stages and by Chaucer's time it had become 'peche'. Presumably it was Pliny's account, written in the first century, that set everybody thinking for 1800 years that the peach came from Persia. He called it the Persian apple and said it was quite safe for invalids to eat and there was no truth in the story that Egyptian kings had administered peaches as punishment because of the excruciating pain they were alleged to cause.

In 1883 a Swiss botanist Alphonse De Candolle threw doubt on the Persian theory and, on literary evidence, deduced that peaches probably came from China. Scientific research and botanical exploration since then have supported this.

The nectarine is a type of peach with a smooth skin. It probably originated as a bud sport on a peach, for nectarines sometimes appear on peach trees or vice versa, while a fruit smooth on one side and hairy on the other has been known. Some peaches are grown as ornamentals (page 99).

Fan-trained Peach tree, *Prunus persica*, growing against a wall

The cultivated pear of Europe, *Pyrus communis*

Pear (Pyrus)

The pear is closely related to the apple and for long both were regarded as belonging to the same genus, *Pyrus*. The main differences are that the styles of the *malus* (apple) blossom are joined at or near the base, the fruit of the apple is globular while that of the pear is more often rounded at one end, tapering towards the other and the flesh of the mature pear contains grit cells which the apple's does not.

In Europe the cultivated pear is descended from *Pyrus communis,* a native of temperate Europe and western Asia as far as the Himalayas. It has become naturalized in Britain. The wild pear (*P. communis*) will grow to 50 feet, is often spiny and lives longer than the apple. If grown on their own roots, the cultivated varieties would reach a similar height but in gardens and many orchards they are grafted on quince roots and their resulting growth is dwarfed.

Pears have been cultivated for thousands of years and have changed remarkably little in that time. Pliny listed thirty-nine varieties, some of which appear to have been remarkably like Williams' Bon Chrétien first grown about 1770 by John Stair, an Aldermaston schoolmaster, and introduced to the public by a Turnham Green nurseryman named Williams. This is the pear now grown in such quantity in America and in Australia for canning, and goes by the name of Bartlett after the Enoch Bartlett who took it across the Atlantic in 1799.

Since Bartlett's time new varieties have been raised in the United States by crossing European pears with the so-called Japanese Sand Pear (*Pyrus pyrifolia*), a native of China. The Sand Pears were so named because of the extremely gritty nature of their flesh. They are good keepers, rounder, more like an apple in shape, but not of good dessert quality.

While pear blossom is pretty enough, no purely ornamental varieties have been cultivated as is the case with apples. Actually pear blossom has a somewhat fishy perfume but this is more likely to be noticed by the two-winged flies which it attracts, rather than by human noses.

Nevertheless some varieties of cultivated pear are notable for the rich autumn colouring of their leaves. Durondeau, Fertility, Souvenir du Congrès and Thompson's are some of these. Just as cider is the alcoholic drink made from apple juice, so is perry the drink made from pear juice.

Japanese Sand Pear,
Pyrus pyrifolia

The cultivated plum,
Prunus domestica

Plum (Prunus)

Other fruits belonging to the genus *Prunus,* apricot and cherry
(pages 110 to 111) and peach and nectarine (pages 118 to 119)
have already been discussed. These fruit, however, have the
classical name 'Prunus' applied to the whole group. Like other
fruits which have long been popular and cultivated in
orchards and gardens for many centuries, the lineage of the
plum is a tangled skein now difficult or impossible to unravel.
The dessert plums of today, as typified by the variety Victoria, seem to have originated in southwest Asia and to have
stemmed from the species botanists now call *Prunus domestica*.

But even *P. domestica* may not be the original parent. There
is a theory that this was the result of a cross between *P.
spinosa* and *P. divaricata*. The former is the Sloe or Blackthorn of English woods, a native of Europe and western Asia.
The latter is very much like the Cherry Plum or Myrobalan
(*P. cerasifera*) from western Asia and the Caucasus, and is
sometimes regarded as a variety of it.

The Wild Plum or Common Plum (*P. domestica*) is found

growing in English woods and hedgerows, forming a round-headed tree some 20 to 30 feet high. Such specimens, however, are believed to be 'garden escapes' that have become naturalized.

The only plum which is a true native of Britain is the Bullace (*P. insititia*) which is much like *P. domestica* but a smaller tree and whereas the fruit of the latter is egg-shaped, black with a bluish bloom, that of the Bullace is round, and purple or yellow. Bullaces have been grown in Europe since prehistoric times.

The Damson is classed as a variety of *P. insititia* but is not native to Britain. It was supposed originally to have come from Damascus and was known as the Damascene Plum which gradually became shortened to 'damson'. The fruit are rather bitter: too astringent to be eaten raw. The preserve made from them is known as 'cheese'. Some of the cultivated varieties of Damson grown today were the product of a marriage between *P. insititia* and a *P. domestica* variety. A close relative of the Damson is the Mirabelle, popular in France but almost unknown in Britain.

The Gage group of plums,

Sloe or Blackthorn, *Prunus spinosa*

Cherry Plum or Myrobalan, *Prunus cerasifera*

White Bullace, *Prunus insititia*

The Damson

Wildgoose Plum, *Prunus munsoniana*

Canada Plum, *Prunus nigra*

(*Above*) the American Plum, *Prunus americana* and (*below*) the Chicasaw Plum, *Prunus angustifolia*

such as the Green Gage, Cambridge Gage, and Transparent Gage, is a rather special one, in that they have a certain characteristic rich flavour all their own and are generally regarded as of the highest dessert quality. Some botanists believe they originated from a cross between *P. domestica* and *P. insititia*, and others think they derive from *italica* a variety of *P. insititia*.

The Green Gage was the first of this class and seems to have appeared in Armenia and spread westwards. Reaching France in the reign of Francis I (1494–1547), it was named Reine Claude after his queen. It reached England in 1724, if not before, and was named Green Gage in honour of Sir William Gage who planted it in his garden at Hengrave Hall, near Bury St Edmunds, Suffolk.

A Chinese species, *P. salicina,* was imported into the United States in 1870 from Japan and a number of varieties produced, misleadingly known as 'Japanese plums'. These bear their flowers in threes and are hardier and more vigorous than *P. domestica,* but the fruit are of inferior flavour.

Several native North American species include the Allegheny Plum (*P. alleghaniensis*), the American Plum (*P. americana*), the Canada Plum (*P. nigra*), the Chickasaw Plum (*P. angustifolia*), the Hortulan Plum (*P. hortulana*) and the Wildgoose Plum (*P. munsoniana*). Ornamental flowering plums are described on page 99.

Quince (Cydonia oblonga)

The Quince is a shallow-rooted, spreading deciduous tree, up to 25 feet high, often with very crooked branches. It has been grown for many centuries around the Mediterranean and in southern England. The golden-yellow fruit are used as flavouring in cooking rather than on their own. Quince is often used as a dwarfing rootstock for pears. Closely akin to *Cydonia oblonga* is the Japanese Quince (*Chaenomeles lagenaria*), a popular wall shrub in England. It has toothed leaves and the fragrant fruit are somewhat rounder than the Quince.

Walnut (Juglans)

The Common Walnut (*Juglans regia*) is the species most widely grown for its nuts and is described on pages 70 and 71.

Tree and fruit of the Quince,
Cydonia oblonga

125

Cultivated varieties of fruit

Popular cultivated varieties of apples. (*Above left*) Bramley's Seedling, (*above right*) Cox's Orange Pippin, (*below left*) Golden Delicious, (*below right*) Discovery. (*Opposite*) 1. Empire ; 2. Granny Smith ; 3. Lord Lambourne ; 4. McIntosh ; 5. Scarlet Pimpernel ; 6. Sturmer Pippin

(*Above*) two other popular varieties of apple, Sunset (*left*) and Worcester Pearmain (*right*). (*Below*) apricots, Moorpark (*left*) and Alfred (*right*). (*Opposite*) four varieties of cherry (*top from left to right*) Noble, Napoleon Bigarreau, Early Rivers, Waterloo; (*centre*) the nectarine Humboldt; (*bottom*) peaches, Rochester (*left*) and Duke of York (*right*)

Cultivated pear varieties:
(*above left*) Doyenné du Comice
(*right*) Beurré Hardy; (*below*)
Conference (*left*) and Williams'
Bon Chrétien (*right*)

Varieties of plum

Coe's Golden Drop

Jefferson

Greengage

Czar

Marjorie's Seedling

Victoria

Hippocrates teaching beneath a
plane tree which outlived him
by 2,300 years

TREES IN HISTORY

To look upon an old tree is to gaze at history. There are trees
growing today which were no longer young when our
civilization began. Such is the General Sherman Tree in
Sequoia National Park, a representative of *Sequoiadendron
giganteum* thought by some experts to be 3,800 years old.

An Oriental Plane (*Platanus orientalis*) under which Hippocrates was supposed to have sat, on the island of Cos, outlived the 'Father of Medicine' by over 2,300 years. But these
are exceptions. There is no trace now of the plane tree at
Lydia in Asia Minor with which Xerxes the Persian king so
fell in love on his way to invade Greece that he jeopardized
his immense army, tarrying beneath its ample shade and
rewarding it with costly gifts of jewelry which he hung from
the branches. Perhaps that single tree knew why the Greeks
could hold him at Thermopylae and defeat him at Salamis.

Often trees with historic associations have been the victims
of their own fame. The mulberry Shakespeare planted in his

garden in 1609 was cut down in 1765 to make into souvenirs, a fate which, in 1801, also met the weeping willow grown from a cutting by Alexander Pope in his Twickenham garden.

One of the most famous of historic trees was the oak in which Charles II hid at Boscobel, in Shropshire, after the battle of Worcester. The tree had been lopped a few years previously which was why it gave the king such good cover but after the Restoration souvenir-hunters removed its great bulk a handful at a time until it expired.

By contrast, an ash tree which is supposed to have sheltered the Duke of Monmouth hiding in a Dorset ditch after the battle of Sedgemoor in 1685, still survives. So, too, does the Heddon Oak, in Somerset from which were hanged men sentenced by the notorious Judge Jeffreys for their part in the rebellion. Monmouth himself was beheaded and when the Duchess heard the news she had all the oaks in her park cut in half so that they might never be of use for the king's ships.

Trees have been planted to commemorate events. The lime avenue at Malvern Hall, Solihull celebrates Waterloo and the clumps of beech near Amesbury Abbey represent the British and French fleets at the start of the Battle of Trafalgar.

Charles II of England hiding from Roundheads in an oak at Boscobel

TREES IN RELIGION

Unfeeling indeed would be he who could walk into a forest of mighty trees and not experience a sense of awe almost akin to reverence. Often the straight boles towering towards the heavens must remind us of the tall stone columns rising to the roof of a mediaeval cathedral.

Our ideas on religion are derived from or influenced by those of our forebears and when the relationship between trees and religion is studied it is found that we are going back to the earliest days of man on Earth. When forests abounded and provided men with shelter, food, medicine and defence from their enemies, it is not surprising that trees assumed a predominant role in their religious beliefs and rites. Many of these ancient ideas still linger on and still affect the lives and behaviour of civilized people today.

The World Tree of Buddhism; Mandara, the tree of the Indian paradise; the Tree of Life; the Tree of Knowledge in the garden of Eden – there are similarities in all these ideas. The Druids attached mystic significance to mistletoe, particularly when it grew upon oak trees – and we still hang bunches from our ceilings at Christmas.

Ceremonial cutting down of mistletoe by Druids in an oak grove

Yews were a pagan symbol of immortality that continued into the Christian era

The ancients made gifts of evergreen boughs at their mid-winter festival and Druids offered winter harbour to the spirit of the trees by placing evergreen branches about their homes. We still decorate our houses with holly and forget that the name is but a corruption of 'holy'.

The Maypole dance is probably a memory of a May Day ceremony round a tree. Old customs such as the horn dance at Abbots Bromley was probably once a pagan rite connected with the oak-cult of Zeus. Some trees were invested by tradition with a sinister aura. Such were the Judas Tree (*Cercis siliquastrum*) from which Judas Iscariot was said to have hanged himself, and the Hawthorn (*Crataegus*) which provided Christ's crown of thorns and therefore was unlucky to cut down.

The popular idea that the aged yews in English churchyards were planted to provide wood for soldiers' bows hardly bears examination. Best bows were always made from imported wood. Yews were revered by the Druids and Christians often built churches near pagan sacred places and in time the old yews were accepted as symbols of immortality.

135

TREES IN LITERATURE AND ART

From the days of mythical Greece until the present, trees have been a source of inspiration for poets and writers.

Fancy may range from the hackneyed ballad 'Trees' to the old music-hall ditty 'Under the Old Apple Tree'. In the opening paragraph to *Under the Greenwood Tree* Thomas Hardy points out that every tree has its voice – the sob of the fir, the hiss of the ash, the rustle of the beech. One may remember also, the imaginary Tumtum Tree in Lewis Carroll's 'Through the Looking Glass'.

In the world of paintings, trees have engaged the powers of the world's greatest artists. John Crome's 'Oak at Poringland' in the London Tate Gallery convincingly conveys the strength of a mighty tree and the etching by Rembrandt 'The Three Trees' conjures up the atmosphere of outdoor grandeur with such economy

(*Above left*) John Crome painting his 'Oak at Poringland' now in the Tate Gallery. (*Left*) totem poles carved by Pacific coast American Indians and (*right*) a totem pole from Queen Charlotte Island

of detail. Splendid trees are found in the works of all the classic landscape painters – Constable, Gainsborough, Cotman, Hobbema, as well as such moderns as Paul Nash, Adrian Bury, Adrian Hill and Ethelbert White.

Trees also play a more direct part in many works of art. Wood-carving is a prime example, as found in the art of primitive peoples, the carved masks and totem poles of the North American Indians for instance, or in the sophisticated handiwork of Grinling Gibbons who sometimes used the smooth, dense, pinkish-brown wood of the pear but always preferred the pale, soft wood of the lime (*Tilia vulgaris*).

Painters' materials, palettes, easels, brush handles and charcoal, all come from trees. The North American Pencil Cedar (*Juniperus virginiana*) is the traditional source of soft timber for pencils. From the kernels of walnuts (*Juglans regia*) an oil may be pressed, said to be the best of all for the preparation of artists' colours. If a log of pine is sawn through, the odour of 'turps', or spirits of turpentine can be recognized. This is distilled from an oily secretion of pine trees.

137

TREES IN SHIP-BUILDING

The first 'boats' were no doubt logs which happened to float. With the invention of tools larger logs were hollowed out and so the first ships were made. One of these early 'canoes' was hauled from the bottom of a lake at Davey Strand between Dublin and Cavan in 1844. Cut from a Durmast Oak (*Quercus petraea*), it was 40 feet long.

Noah was the first ship-builder whose activities were recorded. He was instructed to make the ark from gopher wood, generally thought to be cypress, presumably *Cupressus sempervirens,* the Mediterranean Cypress. The famous Cedars of Lebanon supplied timber for Solomon's temple and the warring fleets of the ancient Assyrians and Persians. By 333 BC Alexander the Great found that all the trees on the southern slopes had been felled. Oak was used by Greeks and Romans for ship-building, and also by the later Norse raiders and for the famous 'wooden walls' of England.

Although the first forest clearances were made for the purposes of agriculture, it was the warring nations' need of timber for building their navies, century after century, which led to the almost complete deforestation of the whole Mediterranean seaboard. In England the timber shortage frightened Nelson and his practical lieutenant Admiral Collingwood carried acorns in his pockets to plant in the hedgerows. Oak was used, too, for trenails ('tree-nails'), the wooden pins used to secure planks to the ribs.

Elm was used for keels of large vessels but not for small ones liable to be pulled out of the water. It is a durable timber if submerged in salt water but decays in damp air. Masts were a problem in England where trees tend to be short and bushy. The difficulty was sometimes overcome by splicing but by 1297 pine masts were being imported from Norway. Students of Samuel Pepys will know the provision of masts for His Majesty's navy was his constant pre-occupation.

(*Opposite top to bottom*) prehistoric man made the first boats by gouging out tree trunks ; Noah's gopher wood ark is supposed to have been made from cypresses ; masts being 'stepped' in Nelson's time – pine trees from Norway were used for centuries.

TREES IN FURNITURE-MAKING

Until the end of the seventeenth century most British furniture was constructed of home-grown oak. This may have been either from the Common Oak (*Quercus robur*) or the Durmast Oak (*Q. petraea*) but this would have made no difference at all to the distinctive figuring of the wood.

Differences in the appearance of the wood result from the way it has grown. The best timber comes from the best land, growing fastest. With slow growth, development of dense summerwood is reduced. Annual rings are closer together and the timber, containing a higher proportion of the more porous springwood is relatively soft and light in weight.

In Britain oak, poplar, willow and elm trees were frequently pollarded. This cutting concentrated the development in the trunk and had a marked effect on the grain of the timber. In France pollarding was also customary with walnut trees.

(*From top to bottom*) wood of the Common Oak ; Jacobean table made in the 'age of oak' ; Common Oak Tree ; Oak veneer

In old furniture there are no metal nails or screws. Oak in fact, contains acids which tend to corrode any metals with which it comes into contact. With iron, the tannin in the wood forms iron tannate which discolours the wood.

Old Tudor and Jacobean furniture was probably made from home-grown timber. In more recent years much oak has been imported from Europe, particularly Poland, the Baltic countries and Czechoslovakia, the latter wood being known as Austrian oak, a heritage of the Austro-Hungarian Empire.

About the middle of the seventeenth century walnut began to be used in furniture-making. As taste demanded more elegant designs, walnut was used both in the solid and as a veneer. English walnut (*Juglans regia*) was used but timber was also imported from France, Italy and further afield. The French walnut is the lightest in colour, paler and greyer than the English. The Italian is darker, rather streaky, and with a quite pronounced figure in it.

(*From top to bottom*) wood of the Common Walnut; the 'age of walnut' represented by a Queen Anne cabinet; Common Walnut Tree; Walnut veneer

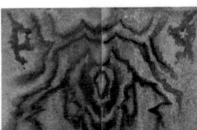

(*From top to bottom, left to right*) a Georgian bureau *circa* 1800 ; *Swietenia mahogani,* one of the two trees that supplies the timber called mahogany : eighteenth century commode with elaborate marquetry ; *Zanthoxylum flavium,* a West Indian tree that provided the yellow wood, known as satin-wood, a popular veneer in the latter half of the eighteenth century ; *Dalbergia latifolia,* one of the several trees that supplies rosewood, used extensively for inlaying

'Satin walnut' is something quite different and is not what it apparently purports to be. This attractive reddish-brown wood, with its satin lustre, is the heartwood from the American Red Gum or Sweet Gum (*Liquidambar styraciflua*) of the south-eastern states of North America.

During the time of William and Mary, and Queen Anne, the general lines of furniture were simple and walnut was the favourite wood. Increasing use was made of veneers and increasingly elaborate patterns were made in marquetry and parquetry, in which the design was built up with veneers of woods of contrasting colour applied to the groundwork.

For all this inlay work a wide range of woods was used, chosen for their attractive and varied colouring, but like satin walnut they often masqueraded under misleading names. Rosewood, for instance, was mentioned by John Evelyn in 1664 as suitable for inlaying – but it has no connection with roses, except that its close-grained wood is fragrant. It came from several species of Dalbergia, especially *D. nigra* from Brazil and *D. latifolia* from the East Indies, and sometimes from the South American Tipu (*Tipuana tipu*).

Species of Dalbergia, too, supplied the wood, lighter in tone than rosewood, which in the seventeenth century was called Prince's Wood or Prince Wood, later Kingwood. This was used as a veneer and in parquetry. Late in the eighteenth century it was used as cross-banding in borders. Tulipwood was another Dalbergia alias. This was imported from Brazil and also used by cabinet-makers in the second half of the eighteenth century in cross-banded borders.

Satinwood was the name for a lustrous, yellow wood originating in several trees, but particularly the West Indian *Zanthoxylum flavium,* and used as a veneer on British furniture from about 1765. Later, the timber from the East Indian *Chloroxylon swietenia* was imported as East Indian satinwood and used for similar purposes until superseded by rosewood.

Mahogany first came into favour in the early Georgian period. True mahogany is either from *Swietenia macrophylla,* a 100-foot evergreen of Central America or *S. mahogani* of the West Indies. Most of the African mahoganies come from *Khaya ivorensis,* a 140-foot giant of the West African rain forests.

TREES IN INDUSTRY

Wood was the first and most obvious raw material available to primitive man. Trees provided him with a roof, fuel to keep him warm and often food to eat. As the use of tools was learned, wood was fashioned into utensils, boats, furniture and countless aids to daily life. From that day to this, wood has been one of the main staples of existence and through the ages there have been many stories of man's resource and courage in adapting wood to the needs of his industry.

In medicine, for instance, there was the long quest for the Peruvian or Fever Bark Tree which cured malaria. This genus was subsequently named *Cinchona* in honour of the Spanish Viceroy of Peru, Count de Cinchon, whose wife was, in 1638, cured of the ague, as malaria was then called, by an infusion of bark obtained from a tree native to Peru. In spite of this success it was long before 'Peruvian Bark' was recognized by the medical profession. Robert Talbor, for instance, was regarded very much as a quack although he cured Charles II of the ague with this South American preparation from the forests and was knighted for his service.

It was even longer before the real identity of the tree supplying the fever bark was established. The trees grew in remote, unexplored jungle. The natives wished to keep their secrets and were suspicious of white men. One botanist, a Frenchman, Joseph Jussieu, spent twenty-five years in the mid-eighteenth century, exploring the forests and studying the Cinchonas, only to have all his specimens and his notebooks stolen by a servant. For ten more years he chased the thief and lost his reason in the process.

It was eventually found that there were some forty species in this genus, all superficially much alike, but varying markedly in their bark and, particularly, its content of the fever-curing alkaloid, which is now known as quinine.

A story more specifically belonging to industry is that of rubber. As far back as the beginning of the sixteenth century Spaniards brought back from Mexico balls of a strange substance obtained from trees. Nothing like it had been seen before. Rubber had been discovered but it was centuries before its commercial significance was realized.

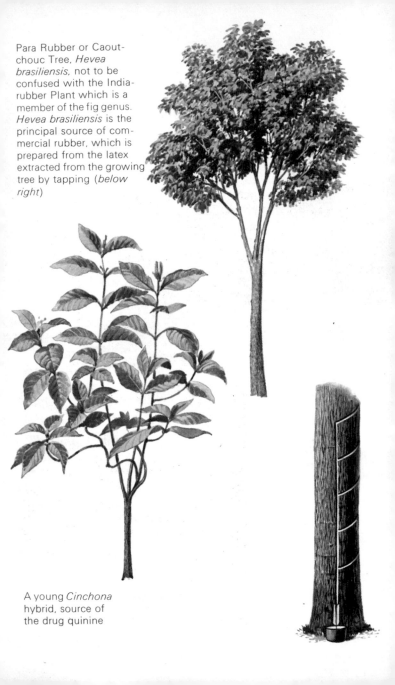

Para Rubber or Caout-
chouc Tree, *Hevea
brasiliensis*, not to be
confused with the India-
rubber Plant which is a
member of the fig genus.
Hevea brasiliensis is the
principal source of com-
mercial rubber, which is
prepared from the latex
extracted from the growing
tree by tapping (*below
right*)

A young *Cinchona*
hybrid, source of
the drug quinine

Canadian conifer forest and pulping plant (*above*). (*Right*) conifer wood pulp is the raw material from which nearly all the paper required in the world today is made.

Rubber can be obtained from the latex or sap of several trees, particularly *Hevea brasiliensis,* which grows to a height of 60 feet along the River Amazon, an area which used to be one of the most inhospitable parts of the world. When methods were found of working this strange black resin, the Brazilian Government, appreciating the value of this natural asset, placed an embargo on the export of seeds.

In 1876 Henry Wickham collected some 70,000 seeds, chartered a cargoless ship on behalf of the Indian Government and somehow managed to evade the Brazilian customs officials. Wickham brought his seeds safely back to Kew and was knighted for his exploit. From this consignment 2,700 plants were successfully raised and in due course sent to Ceylon in Wardian cases. From those trees stemmed the vast rubber industry in Malaya, Indonesia, Ceylon, India and Burma.

One of the economic difficulties of adjusting afforestation policies to meet man's needs, is the slow growth of a tree compared with the rapid changes in needs brought about by man's inventiveness. The Spanish conquistadors who bounced their rubber balls had no idea of mackintoshes, galoshes, wellington boots or motor-car tyres.

Daniel Defoe, of *Robinson Crusoe* fame, toured England and Wales in 1724 and saw no danger in the widespread felling of oak trees in Sussex to provide fuel and charcoal for the iron foundries. He thought the forests constituted 'one inexhaustible store-house of timber never to be destroyed, but by a general conflagration, and able at this time to supply timber to rebuild all the royal navies of Europe'.

Eighty years later the 'inexhaustible store-house' was nearly exhausted and Lord Nelson was seriously worried about the ships of the future. The trees from the acorns Collingwood planted were not due for felling until the time of World War I, some sixty years after the first ironclads.

The first paper was probably made in Egypt from papyrus, a reed pith. The Chinese used the bark of mulberry trees or bamboo shoots. The Arabs introduced rag which gave strength and for centuries most paper was made from this material. By the middle of the nineteenth century it was obvious that the rag supply was insufficient and the hunt began for substitutes.

Many trees have to be felled each year to provide supports in mines

Wood is composed of cellulose fibres held together by nature's plastic, a substance called lignin. By breaking the wood down mechanically and then heating it either with an acid (the sulphite process) or with an alkali (the sulphate process), the lignin is removed and the remaining cellulose becomes paper. Wood pulp was first used in 1873; today it is the raw material for very nearly all the paper in the world. Conifers are used for this purpose because their fibres are longer than those of the hardwood trees.

Apart from its major use for constructional purposes and as fuel for heating, wood has many valuable by-products – charcoal, pitch, wood creosote, tannin, dyestuffs, essential oils, to mention a few. During this century other uses for the cellulose constituent of wood, apart from paper, have been discovered. Hundreds of tons of pulpwood are now used annually in the manufacture of viscose rayon and cellulose packaging film. Most of this comes from the conifers of North America and Scandinavia, but, in Britain, more than a quarter of the pulp for this purpose comes from *Eucalyptus saligna*, an Australian native now grown in South Africa.

'Reconstructed timber', that is plywood, insulating and hardboards, and photographic films, adhesives, lacquers and nitro-cellulose explosives are other wood products. Sugars, alcohol and yeast for animal feeding are all obtained from cellulose and in World War II these processes were very important, although in peace time cost is still against them.

The lignin extracted from the wood still appears to be rather a waste-product and its exact chemical nature and behaviour still something of a mystery. When lignin yields up all its secrets it could well prove the key to new wood products as yet undreamed of.

It is ironic that so many man-hours are spent digging coal from the ground and millions of trees have to be grown to provide mine props to hold up the honeycomb of excavations made. Until quite recently the mining industry was easily the largest single buyer of home-grown timber in Britain.

What is mined can never be replaced but new trees can be grown to replace those felled. Could there be a stronger case for planting more trees and for more research so that better use can be made of those cut down? After all wood, like coal, is only an elaborate combination of water and carbon.

Timber props stacked at a colliery

GLOSSARY

A few of the technical terms used and not fully described within the text:

Angiosperm: plants which produce seeds enclosed in an outer casing. This group is sub-divided into **monocotyledons** and **dicotyledons**

Anther: see **stamen**

Aril: an outer covering of a seed. The hard-coated seed of the Common Yew, for instance, is enclosed in a fleshy cup (the aril) which becomes bright red by the autumn

Berry: a fruit in which the seed is protected only by a layer of soft flesh

Bract: a modified leaf growing on a flower stalk, outside sepals and petals, or from the axil from which the flower springs

Calyx: the outer part of a flower which encloses the petals and reproductive organs. The constituent parts of the calyx are called **sepals**. The calyx protects the flower bud

Carpel: the ovule-bearing female part of a flower at its centre

Corolla: inside the calyx comes a ring of petals, often coloured. Collectively, these petals form the corolla

Cotyledon: a seed leaf – the first leaf to grow from the seed and usually simpler in outline than the leaves formed later

Dicotyledon: a plant with a pair of seed leaves. Most of the broad-leaved trees belong to this group

Dioecious: term applied to plants in which the flowers are unisexual, the sexes being on separate plants

Drupe: a fruit in which the seed is encased in a hard wall, the stone, and then in a layer of flesh

Fastigiate: of erect, close-growing habit, rather like a bundle of twigs in a broom

Figure: the pattern in wood resulting from differences of colour variations between sapwood and heartwood

Filament: see **stamen**

Genus: (pl. **genera**): see page 5

Glabrous: smooth, without hairs

Glaucous: bluish or greyish green, often used to indicate a white bloom as is found on black grapes

Grain: the direction in which the fibres of wood run; thus,

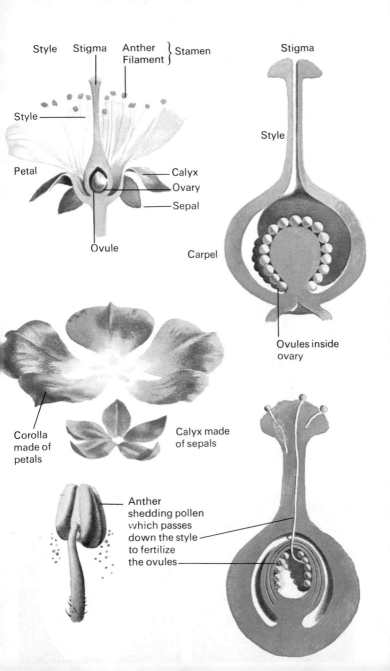

Style   Stigma   Anther } Stamen
          Filament }

Style

Stigma

Style

Petal

Calyx
Ovary
Sepal

Ovule

Carpel

Ovules inside
ovary

Corolla
made of
petals

Calyx made
of sepals

Anther
shedding pollen
which passes
down the style
to fertilize
the ovules

(*Left from top to bottom*) example of straight grain; crooked grain deviations caused by knots; patterns of this type are constructed by cabinet makers with veneers. (*Right top*) overall pattern of a piece of wood is called a figure. (*Below*) types of fruit or seed vessel:
1. Aril; 2. Berry; 3. Drupe; 4. Pome

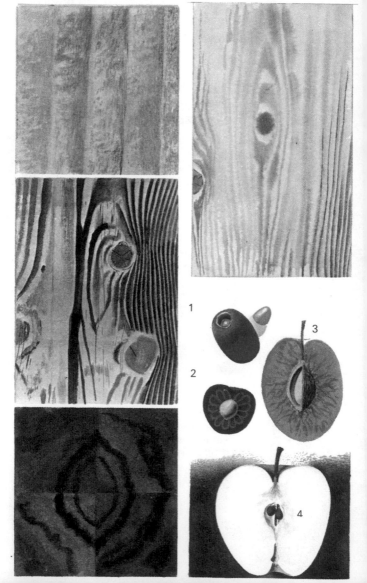

'straight grain' means that they are all parallel to the vertical surface of the trunk. Knots cause irregularities in the grain. The general patterning is known as the **figure**

Gymnosperm: the opposite of angiosperm. They produce their seeds unenclosed in an ovary. Conifers are in this class

Hardwood: although in common usage, a hardwood is a heavy, close-grained wood as found in a deciduous tree, as compared with the lighter, soft wood of the conifers. Botanically the terms hardwood and **softwood** describe the cell-structure of the timber itself. The angiosperms contain all the hardwood trees and the gymnosperms all the softwoods.

Monocotyledon: a plant with a single seed leaf. Palms are the most common members of this class

Ovary: the part inside the carpel where the ovules become seeds after fertilization

Ovule: the tiny embryo-seed before it has been fertilized by pollen

Phyllode: a flattened leaf-like extension of a leaf-stalk

Pinetum: a collection of conifers, not necessarily pines

Pome: a fruit produced by several carpels, all enclosed in a layer of flesh, as in the apple

Samara: a flat, winged seed-vessel, as produced by the ash, elm and maple, including the sycamore

Sessile: stalkless

Softwood: see **hardwood**

Species: see page 5

Sport: a spontaneous change from the normal character in a plant or part of a plant. Thus, a peach tree occasionally sports and produces a fuzz-less peach i.e. a nectarine. Sports must be propagated vegetatively

Stamen: the male organ of a flower. It consists of a thin stem, the filament, supporting at its tip the anther which produces the pollen to fertilize the ovules

Stigma: the tip of the style. When the ovules are ready to be fertilized, the stigma usually becomes sticky so as to hold the pollen falling on it

Stoma (pl. **stomata**): a tiny breathing hole in the surface of a leaf or young stem

Style: the extension from the ovary which supports the stigma

Royal Botanic Gardens, Kew, England

PLACES TO VISIT

Below is a list of some of the world's leading arboreta and botanic gardens

Australia
Adelaide Botanic Garden, South Australia
Brisbane Botanic Garden, Queensland
Melbourne Botanic Gardens, South Yarra, Victoria
Sydney Botanic Garden, New South Wales

Britain
National Pinetum, Bedgebury, Kent
University Botanic Garden, Cambridge
Royal Botanic Garden, Edinburgh
Royal Botanic Gardens, Kew, Richmond, Surrey
Wakehurst Place, Sussex
Westonbirt Arboretum, near Tetbury, Gloucestershire
Royal Horticultural Society's Gardens, Wisley, Ripley, Surrey

Canada
Dominion Arboretum, Ottawa
Montreal Botanical Garden, Montreal
Ireland
Castlewellan Forest Park, County Down, Northern Ireland
National Botanic Gardens, Glasnevin, Dublin
New Zealand
Albert Park, Auckland
Botanic Gardens, Christchurch
Botanic Gardens, Dunedin
Kaingaroa State Forest, Rotorua
Pukekura Park, New Plymouth
Waipoua Kauri Forest, Northland
Botanical Gardens, Wellington
United States of America
Arnold Arboretum, Harvard University, Jamaica Plain, Massachusetts
Highland and Durand-Eastman Parks, Rochester, New York
Missouri Botanical Garden, Gray Summit, St Louis, Missouri
Morton Arboretum, Lisle, Illinois
National Arboretum, Washington, DC
University of Washington Arboretum, Seattle, Washington

Sydney Botanic Garden, New South Wales, Australia

INDEX

BOOKS TO READ

Trees and Shrubs Hardy in the British Isles by W. J. Bean (7th Edit. 3 vols.) (8th, New Edit., first volume, June, 1970). John Murray, London, 1950–51.

Trees – a Guide to the Trees of Great Britain and Europe by J. Bretaudeau. Paul Hamlyn, 1967.

The Identification of Trees and Shrubs by F. K. Makins. Dent, 1952.

British Trees by Miles Hadfield. Dent 1957.

British Trees and Shrubs by R. D. Meikle, (The Kew Series). Eyre and Spottiswoode, London, 1958.

Living Trees of the World by T. H. Everett. Thames & Hudson, 1969.

England's Forests by H. L. Edlin. Faber, 1958.

Guide to Tree-Planting and Cultivation by H. L. Edlin. Collins, 1970.

Trees, Woods and Man by H. L. Edlin. Collins, 1966.

SOME OTHER TITLES IN THIS SERIES

- Arts
- Domestic Animals and Pets
- Domestic Science
- Gardening
- General Information
- History and Mythology
- Natural History
- Popular Science

Arts
Antique Furniture/Architecture/Clocks and Watches/Glass for Collectors/Jewellery/Musical Instruments/Porcelain/Victoriana

Domestic Animals and Pets
Budgerigars/Cats/Dog Care/Dogs/Horses and Ponies/Pet Birds/Pets for Children/Tropical Freshwater Aquaria/Tropical Marine Aquaria

Domestic Science
Flower Arranging

Gardening
Chrysanthemums/Garden Flowers/Garden Shrubs/House Plants/Plants for Small Gardens/Roses

General Information
Aircraft/Arms and Armour/Coins and Medals/Flags/Guns/Military Uniforms/National Costumes of the world/Rockets and Missiles/Sailing/Sailing Ships and Sailing Craft/Sea Fishing/Trains/Veteran and Vintage Cars/Warships

History and Mythology
Age of Shakespeare/Archaeology/Discovery of: Africa/The American West/Australia/Japan/North America/South America/Myths and Legends of: Africa/Ancient Egypt/Ancient Greece/Ancient Rome/India/The South Seas/Witchcraft and Black Magic

Natural History
The Animal Kingdom/Animals of Australia and New Zealand/Animals of Southern Asia/Bird Behaviour/Birds of Prey/Butterflies/Evolution of Life/Fishes of the world/Fossil Man/A Guide to the Seashore/ Life in the Sea/Mammals of the world/Monkeys and Apes/Natural History Collecting/The Plant Kingdom/Prehistoric Animals/Seabirds/Seashells/Snakes of the world/Trees of the world/Tropical Birds/Wild Cats

Popular Science
Astronomy/Atomic Energy/Chemistry/Computers at Work/The Earth/Electricity/Electronics/Exploring the Planets/The Human Body/Mathematics/Microscopes and Microscopic Life/Undersea Exploration/The Weather Guide